Opioid Epidemic

Opioid Epidemic

A NATIONAL PLAN TO STOP IT

● ● ●

Terence G. Schiller, MD

ISBN-13: 9781983582370
ISBN-10: 1983582379
Library of Congress Control Number: 2018900383
CreateSpace Independent Publishing Platform
North Charleston, South Carolina

To Linda, the wind in my sails.

Preface

● ● ●

SUBSTANCE ABUSE IN AMERICA KILLS a busload of fifty young people every eight hours and forty-five minutes. Do you know a young person who is getting on this bus? Do you know how to stop this? Do you know who is driving the bus?

I do.

I question everything. I want proof. I want to see the data for myself. I need proof that my next step is one in the right direction, the proper thing to do. I want to see all the details, and I want to see the big picture also. I check everything I do, two or three times before I commit to action. You might call me obsessive compulsive for doing this. But wait, what if I'm your doctor checking on your medical care. Than a personality disorder becomes a desirable trait doesn't it.

First do no harm. That's the oath I took, that we all took, every medical student. I've been called a skeptic, and I accept this as a compliment. I'm skeptical about why young people die in our streets and neighborhoods. I've become obsessed and compulsive about finding a root cause for this loss of lives and searching for ways to stop it. In doing so I have uncovered shortcomings in our country's medical system that contribute to drug abuse and the ultimate loss of lives it causes. We have lost sight of the first and foremost principle of practicing medicine, and we are doing harm. This book is about those shortcomings—the harm they cause and how to resolve them.

I propose a comprehensive plan, from control of children's exposure to substances of abuse, control of pharmaceutical companies, control of doctors, control of use of substances of abuse, to recommendations for future research and development, legislative changes, and the engineering of roadblocks to substance abuse, because no one should die this way.

Terence Schiller, MD, FightDrugsNow@gmail.com

If you are reading this, you are as interested in stopping this needless loss of young lives as I am. I am a medical doctor. I have seen fights for life won and lost, but nothing has affected me as much as the thought of young people dying without my intervention. I am also an engineer. I left my sixteen-year engineering career to go to medical school. Before that I worked in construction and served an apprenticeship with the US Navy. I have seen many types of tough problems solved by research, planning, design, and teamwork. I have learned from navy ship captains to brick masons, from drug addicts to ministers. I have been contacting government officials for ten years with my proposals to stop loss of life from substance abuse. During these ten years, I have watched the yearly death toll more than double (data from 2017 reporting 64,000 overdose deaths and about 23,500 in year 2000.) And my letters have gotten no response from representatives, senators, two presidents, attorneys general, or health secretaries.

This volume provides an extensive introduction to my thought process in drafting my national plan. I will take you from the basics of the problem—definition, analysis of types of problem solving, application of problem-solving methods, with simple examples—all the way to detailed plans on how to stop the destruction of life brought on by substance abuse, with your newly acquired problem-solving skills and your passion to do good.

I don't know what to say to inspire your faith and trust in me enough to read this complicated document. It is difficult reading and will take time. Perhaps a short story will help. One day I was very busy in the office, with tons of people in the waiting room. All the patients' cases were complicated; there was nothing simple that day. At one point, the office manager went into the lobby and announced that I was very busy and that it would be two hours before the next person was seen. After waiting for a response, she came back and told me that no one left. Those persons felt my opinion was worth waiting two hours for. That was their decision. I hope I provide a clear enough concept for you to agree with them, after you read this book.

The problem of substance abuse is large and complex. There is no simple solution. There are people who profit from substance abuse, and they are not just drug dealers. Anyone who is involved in this problem on either side and draws an income from it profits. Now, I am not saying that anyone who gets a paycheck for fighting drugs is bad. But I am saying that you and I must be on guard that maximum effort is made in prevention. Yes, treatment is needed and vital. But we must make our first priority the prevention of a problem. The next priority is treatment. We must guard against government officials who spend only for treatment and not for prevention or spend more for treatment than prevention. Do you want your child to be treated for drug addiction or to never become addicted to begin with by good prevention? The answer is simple. Please ask yourself, "What is my government doing, prevention or treatment?"

DEFINING THE PROBLEM

A problem poorly defined is seldom solved. Without clear definition of a problem, one cannot likely develop a solution to it. For example, when you learned math, you may have thought that the "word problems" were hard because you had to know the math and you had to develop a math problem by reading the question. The substance-abuse problem seems concise, but it's not. Some think it's just a result of bringing other countries' heroin into the United States and young people getting addicted to the drug and overdosing on it. But it's not that simple. If it were that simple, then all we would have to do is build a wall around the country and the problem would stop. Many persons opposed to this line of thinking feel that's not going to work. We need far more than stopping the import of foreign drugs to prevent drug addiction. I will show you how to clearly define the problem. Later you will see analysis. But the main concept to absorb when defining this problem is that more than half of the drug deaths in this country are from drugs manufactured here in the United States. Saying that Mexico is the whole problem is absolutely wrong.

What Is Our Present State?

Understanding our present condition is also crucial. There is a huge difference between being in a place that is not where you want to be and being lost. If you don't know where you are now, then you are lost. If I'm sailing off the coast of New York and I want to be in New Jersey, then all I have to do is sail south to New Jersey. But if I'm lost—now, that's different. I don't know what to do next. So what is our present position on drug overdoses in the United States?

Simply put, we are losing the battle. In the past ten years, drug-overdose deaths have more than doubled. This means that whatever we are doing is *not working*. I have said this to many public officials, and they seem to take offense at it. This is not an insult; it's just an observation that, in some cases, the same measures have been taken for ten years with no results. They may be profiting from this problem or they don't care or they just need more help from the public, from someone like me. You be the judge.

In our present state, we are losing terribly. We are now losing American lives to substance abuse at nearly the same rate that we lost lives to battle in World War II and nearly twenty times as fast as we did in the Vietnam War. Please absorb this paragraph. There are more statistics to come.

Problem-Solving Skills

As I stated above, I want to show you some fundamental problem-solving skills and then apply them to the problem of substance abuse—in particular, to the problem of drug-abuse deaths. First and foremost, let's stop the deaths.

Why Would an Intelligent, Hardworking Person Not Want to Solve a Problem?

If the problem is incorrectly defined, then the solution will not address the real problem.

I divide a problem-based situation into: (A) the correct solution to the problem, which is the same as saying the correct solution to the correctly defined problem; (B) the wrong correct solution to the problem, which is the same as the correct solution to the wrongly defined problem. Also, both type A and type B solutions can be applied to a single part of the problem, which again will not solve the whole problem. You can think of this as types of solutions—A-complete, A-partial, B-complete, and B-partial—or mixes of the solution types, if we are dealing with a multi-faceted problem. Later I will show you how to further break down types of solutions into three more categories. Then you can use this system for all your complex problem-solving tasks.

In summary, we have four types of problems:

    A—correctly defined problem
    B—poorly defined problem
    C—completely defined problem or problem list
    P—partly defined problem

We also have four types of solutions: A-C, A-P, B-C, and B-P.

Later, I'll show you three subcategories, so we will have twelve types of solutions to problems. When we reanalyze drug-overdose deaths with these new skills, you may actually love the full set of type A solutions we eventually develop.

Let me give you some examples. These examples will start with extreme made-up situations and move to subtler real problems that I have seen. I have not selected any highly technical engineering or medical problems, as they would require too much introduction.

Example 1: A simplistic fictional example to learn with.

A small child reaches into a kitchen drawer that is too high for him to clearly see into and accidentally cuts himself on a knife. The father must spend all night in the ER with the child, who is getting stitches to close the cut, and some days at home, tending to his son, and time in another ER visit to have the stitches removed. So to prevent all that wasted time and money, he goes on the Internet, where he learns to suture, and he buys sutures so that he can do the procedure himself next time.

Pretty simple example, isn't it? Clearly, it's the right solution to the wrong problem. The problem is the placement of the knives, not the stitches. The dad viewed the problem as having to go to the ER. The problem is the child's access to knives. To prevent a cut, the dad simply has to put the knives in a place where the child does not have access to them. Prevention of the accident is the preferred solution.

Example 2: Another fictional example.

A house catches fire due to an improperly wired electrical circuit. The community leaders then require a fire extinguisher in every house.

This sounds fine and acceptable. But clearly electrical inspection and smoke detectors could have prevented the fire. And one fire extinguisher is not likely to stop a house fire if the occupants are not warned when the fire is small, as a smoke detector would do. So, in this example, things get a lot more complex. We can invoke electrical inspections, smoke detectors or other types of fire inspections, building codes, fire alarms that connect to police and fire departments, and more. Thus we can address many aspects of prevention and treatment of fires.

Example 3:

This is real. A company changes from using handwritten information to entering information into their computer and printing it out. This makes a big improvement in the ability to change and print information. But the printing is so small that many complain they can't see it. In response, the company gives all the employees a magnifying glass.

Yes, this is a real example—clearly some type of correct solution but to a wrongly defined problem.

More Types of Answers: Engineering versus Administrative Answers

Now let's examine the three types of correct solutions to correctly defined problems that I promised you. In engineering project management, we call these "engineering answers," "administrative answers," or "combined [both engineering and administrative] answers."

So your spouse and children are planning a long drive. They have alternate routes. One route has a large highway with no median strip. There are "No Passing" signs to help prevent head-on collisions. The other route has a toll highway that's similar, but it has a concrete dividing wall that clearly prevents head-on collisions. Which one would you want them to drive on? The concrete wall was designed by engineers to stop all head-on collisions. It's expensive and took time to make, so you must pay a toll. This is the engineering solution to head-on collision problems. The signs were designed by administrative government-type persons with good intent, but people don't obey them, and head-on collisions still occur. Thus we see "engineering" versus "administrative" answers to a dangerous problem.

Here's another example: The electric company is building a high-powered switch station in your town next to the school ball fields. An electrical shock from a stray wire would kill a person. So how do we make it safe?

One proposal is to put up many signs that say, "High Voltage: Keep Out," so that people would know to stay away. Another proposal is to build a high fence with barbed wire to keep people like your children out. Which is the engineering answer, and which is the administrative one? Usually we will do both the fence and the signs.

Walk around any big city, and you will find engineering answers to prevent bad human behavior. Examples include fences, turnstiles, and a subtle one called "hostile architecture" or "disciplinary/defensive architecture," which are those pointy things that you can't sit or walk on.

Now look very carefully at these two examples above. In both cases the engineering answer is clearly the response we want. But they come with a cost and a risk—yes, two things: cost and risk. The cost is money; engineering answers are lifetime solutions, and they cost money. Engineering answers also have some small risk. In the case of the concrete wall, an ambulance cannot cross the highway to be near an accident victim or turn around and go the other way. In the case of the fence, we use barbed wire as the last, albeit dangerous, means of deterring certain death from electrical shock. The concept at play here is accepting a smaller risk to stop a certain larger danger. We will see this in my drug plan, too.

We are all protected by invisible engineering answers every day. Every time you use an automatic teller to take money out of your account, the computer checks whether you have enough to fund the withdrawal. Every time you use your credit card, a computer checks to see whether you have enough credit to make the purchase. The bank protects its money down to the penny with engineering answers to the problem of withdrawing too much. If your bank kept your savings-account money out on a shelf with your name on it so that only you could open the bag, would you consider it safe? Of course not: you expect cash to be in a safe at the bank—another engineering solution/answer to people stealing your money. So remember this: your money is in a safe at the bank, and your automatic-teller computer will not let you get one single penny more than you have.

Where is your narcotic pain medicine, and what controls how much you can have?

· · ·

So now you are familiar with

- correctly defining a problem,
- incorrectly defining a problem,
- partial solutions, and
- complete solutions,

with answers divided into

- engineering answers,
- administrative answers, and
- combined engineering and administrative answers

Amounting to twelve types of final answers in all. And we want complete solutions—in the form of engineering answers—to correctly defined problems for all our problem-solving needs.

APPLYING OUR NEW PROBLEM-SOLVING SKILLS TO DRUG OVERDOSES

This is a very big, complex problem with many aspects to it and many types of drug users. For a variety of reasons, I want to start by working up to the point at which one becomes a drug addict. Beyond that, we would be talking about rehab and the psychology of the addict. In other words, my plan, at this point, is not to address rehab but to prevent (1) the development of addiction, (2) access to drugs, and (3) the distribution of information on how to abuse drugs.

Remember that in my introduction, I stated that preventing drug abuse is preferable to first permitting it and then trying to rehab addicts. I asked, "What is our government doing: prevention or treatment?" My plan addresses the prevention of addiction. I hope to work on a presentation of rehab and treatment and the psychosocial aspects of the drug addict in the future.

Now, to start applying the problem-solving system to the problem of drug-overdose deaths, we start by analyzing and defining the problem. It takes attitude, and mine is one of confidence. This is a problem created by humans, so humans can solve it. Oxycodone and Xanax don't grow on trees. People make them. So let's rip this problem open and look inside.

How big is it? We are now pushing sixty-four thousand deaths per year. To put it in perspective, understand that we lost fifty-eight thousand people in all twenty years of the Vietnam War. Imagine a busload of fifty people going off a cliff and all the people dying, every eight to nine hours. Imagine gunmen coming to every four-year-college graduation and killing twenty kids at each school every year. These bus accidents and graduation slaughters would be all over the news. There were violent protests during the Vietnam era, but now we have twenty times as many people dying and not a single march on Washington. We are losing the lives of young people just about as fast as in World War II; if you add in the violence and accidents that often erupt among intoxicated individuals, then you may find that we exceed the death rate of World War II. Some common cancers do not kill this many people.

Again, how big is this problem? It's very, very big!

Let's start dissecting and defining. Which drugs concern us? Consider these facts:

1) More than half of all drug-related deaths are actually from prescription drugs made in the United States. That is, they are prescription drugs leading directly to death by overdose. Veterinary drugs are being used now, too.
2) About three-eighths of such deaths are of people who became addicted to prescription drugs and then moved on to street drugs.
3) Only one-eighth of the deaths are of persons who started with street drugs.

So seven-eighths of the deaths are of persons who got hooked on prescription drugs. Are you surprised? Now you can start to see how important it is to define the problem correctly. The addictive behavior of seven-eighths of the persons who died because of drugs was initiated by our medical system. And you are hearing this from a doctor.

Now we have nailed three small parts of our problem definition. It gets very complex from here to define the problem in detail, let alone come up with a solution. We must dissect the relationship of everyone involved, again concentrating on what leads up to addiction—that is, the steps that we will want to stop in order to prevent drug addiction. Who are the drug environment players? Ask yourself, "Is there one government agency involved in the whole problem?" The cast of players includes the following:

1) Drug users
2) Drug pushers
3) Pharmaceutical companies
4) Legal drug manufacturers
5) Illegal drug manufacturers
6) Drug inventers
7) The US patent office, which holds drug patents
8) Government agencies that are involved
    8-1) National Institute on Drug Abuse (NIDA)
    8-2) Food and Drug Administration (FDA)
    8-3) National Institutes of Health (NIH)
    8-4) Substance Abuse and Mental Health Services Association (SAMHSA)
    8-5) Drug Enforcement Agency (DEA)
    8-6) American Medical Association (AMA)
    8-7) State run- Prescription Monitoring Programs (PMP) systems
9) Police
10) Lawyers
11) Elected officials

Let's look even more deeply at more aspects of this drug-epidemic problem. Ask yourself as you read all this: "Have I heard any government leaders discussing all these aspects or offering plans to address all these aspects of the drug-overdose problem?"

SUPPLY AND DEMAND

Substances of abuse are just like any other product. Addicts shop around, look for good prices, and try new things. If one product gets expensive, they will try another. So the laws of supply and demand in legitimate business apply to our problem drug market. If the government stops the trade of one illegal product, the suppliers, addicts, and pushers will look for others. Suppression of distribution of one substance of abuse will cause an increase in sales of any other substance that is not being suppressed. We will discuss further how this pattern comes into play when a government does a poor job of defining the total drug-market problem.

GATEWAY DRUGS

In the 1960s, automobile manufacturers invented what they called "pony cars." These were small, inexpensive cars to attract young car buyers, and companies manufactured them because they knew that people tended to stay with the same car manufacturer for most of their lives if they liked their first cars. The small, cheap car was the gateway the company wanted you to go to and through.

We have gateway drugs that young people try. If they have pleasant experiences with those drugs, some go on to stronger, more dangerous drugs and get addicted. You can easily do your own research online and look for studies by government agencies, in PubMed or other sources, to learn which are the gateway drugs.

STREET VERSUS ILLEGAL DRUGS

Today we know that many drug addicts start with prescription drugs and then move on to illegal drugs. The illegal drugs are often cheaper. But let's learn and remember the math of prescription drugs. Look at this example: Many persons who have bad pain from back injuries can work up to and find a doctor who will give them prescriptions for long-acting oxycodone, eighty milligrams (mg) twice or three times per day, and short-acting, ten milligrams three times a day. That's eighty-one hundred milligrams per month. This drug can be sold for up to a dollar per milligram. Even if you pay for your own insurance or pay cash for the doctor visit, you can make a nice profit selling oxycodone. Do you earn eight thousand dollars a month? Try doing your own math: what if you go to a different doctor in each of four states and receive a prescription? Both price and ease of acquisition will influence which drug a person will get. In business they call this "product elasticity."

Imported versus Domestic Drugs

The relationship of imported versus domestic with regard to drugs is no different than it is for any other product type. If you can get a good product cheaper from an importer, you will do so. Transportation and distribution cost affects imported products more than domestic ones, but not by much—just like any other product we buy. However, when importing illegal drugs, suppliers want the products to be as small as possible, to hide them from inspectors and authorities. So if they can make more potent narcotic drugs to fit into smaller places, they will do so. The drug pushers and users also like small products they can hide in their pockets. Thus developed the great push for extremely potent, more concentrated drugs, which can make a slight dosing error profoundly deadly. Can your government make a mistake and contribute to more potent, smaller drugs? Yes, it can. Government action will be met by reaction from those who embrace product elasticity, the illegal drug makers and dealers. More on this later.

Persons Who Profit from This Drug Epidemic

It's sad but true that, sometimes, good people profit when bad things happen. In the case of our drug epidemic, owners of drug rehabs can profit. Of course, we want to rehab our addicts, but we would rather not have them become addicts to begin with. I believe that we are pushed for the development of and spending a lot on rehab and not enough on prevention efforts. The result has been *no improvement*. The death toll increasing every year indicates that our present efforts are not working. Just think, we have more jails than retraining centers, don't we? The persons who oversee apprehension, punishment, incarceration, and rehab often have the inside track on getting government money and support. But those in charge of prevention are often smaller, less vocal groups. Who's overseeing prevention? How about schools, civic groups, religious groups, scouting clubs, parents—you name it—anyone getting young people involved in good activity is helping prevent drug abuse. So if a political official makes laws requiring funding for rehab centers, this may sound good. But if this official or the official's family members or friends own rehab centers, he or she may not be the proper person to oversee this decision-making.

I think such emphasis on rehab could be like "not seeing the forest for the trees." This occurs when we concentrate on the problem that is in front of us without noticing what's behind the problem, which is causing it—in other words, the bigger picture. Are your elected officials addressing the development of the addicts or just addressing the final process of drug rehab?

The Role of Pharmaceutical Companies

We all have cell phones, and we have all seen them get better and better over the years. Cell phone companies are constantly redesigning and improving them, as is the case with TVs and other currently popular products. Well, let me ask you, does the same hold true for pain medicines? Have pain medicines gotten better or just stronger? Nothing has been done to make safer pain meds, only stronger ones. In my plan, you will read about what I believe big industry should be doing with pain-medicine development and why the industry giants should pay for it themselves.

One company reportedly hired twenty-five hundred doctors to travel around the country teaching other doctors that their narcotic is safe and rarely addictive. What do you think about that? We need to control the marketing of any medicine that could be dangerous or addicting.

The foundation for this control is proper study of the medicine leading to correct indication for the prescribing and marketing of it. The plan line items 39 and 31 provide this foundation. To a lesser extent items 32 and 34 are involved in leading to proper marketing too.

The aggressive and misleading marketing of narcotics is now legendary. Many government-sponsored lawsuits have won over these companies and are still ongoing. An authoritative single publication about this is published on line by the National Institute of Health. (First seen in the *American Journal of Public Health 2009 February;99(2):221-227.* It's titled, "The Promotion and Marketing of OxyContin: Commercial Triumph, Public Health Tragedy." The company "conducted more than 40 national pain management and speaker-training conferences at resorts in Florida, Arizona, and California. More than 5,000 physicians, pharmacists, and nurses attended these all-expense paid symposia, where they were recruited and trained for [the company's] speaker bureau." The Drug Enforcement Agency reported that distribution of promotional items to health-care providers was "unprecedented for schedule-II opioids." The company trained its sales force to say that the risk of addiction was less than 1 percent. Later in 2007 three company executives pled guilty to criminal charges of misbranding and paid $634 million in fines. According to the publication in 2001/2002 sales reached $3 billion. This would put sales into tens of billions by the time of the fine. So the fine seems to be a mere 6 percent. This company distributed fifteen thousand copies of a video about oxycontin to doctors without submitting it to the FDA for approval. Later, when the FDA reviewed a second video, they concluded that the video made unsubstantiated claims regarding the benefits to patients.

In this same publication, you will see that according again to government studies by SAMHSA, "Most abusers of prescription opioids get their diverted drugs directly from a doctor's prescription or from prescriptions of friends and family." This NIH/APHA (American Public Health Association) publication has much more revealing information. It's available on line.

Another company reportedly has suggested that when a new narcotic is invented, we should take the old one off the market. This action would make pain sufferers pay more for new name-brand medicine instead of cheaper generic medicine. I heard a political official say that he thought this would help reduce drug abuse. This would only benefit the drug manufacturer making the new medicine, not the pain-suffering patient who will now have to pay more for name-brand medicine. An example is found in a publication by Crews and Denson ("Recovery of Morphine From a

Controlled-Release Preparation" *Cancer* 1990; 62:2642–2644) that prior to the widespread abuse of OxyContin, MS Contin was abused. This shows that abusers will find any available narcotic generic morphine or name brand. Again, watch out for anyone who profits from drug abuse and use and politicians who seek advice from them.

We have talked about many aspects of the drug epidemic, defining it more clearly and evaluating the players. Briefly, we discussed these aspects:

- The size of the problem
- The lack of organized protest about the lives lost (e.g., compared to Vietnam)
- The persons and groups involved
- The major role of prescription drugs: as high as 87 percent of addicts start with them.
- Supply versus demand
- The need to remain critical of persons who profit from drugs and drug abuse
- Product elasticity with regard to drugs
- The role of pharmaceutical companies
- Immoral marketing strategies with regard to narcotics
- The involvement of many government agencies, with *no one* in charge

What you are about to read over the next forty or so pages is the plan I have been mailing, for ten years, to representatives, senators, two presidents, attorneys general, and the secretary of Health and Human Services. In all that time, I have only received one response that indicated to me that my plan was read, from Senator Tim Kaine. He shared his own frustration with the status of efforts to help stop drug abuse.

You will find below a sample letter and details of my plan. Apply the problem-solving skills detailed above while reading the plan, and note the presence of engineering answers in it. Not all solutions are clear engineering answers, but the nationwide computer control on scheduled drugs certainly is. And that computer system would be used in several of the thirty-nine points in the plan.

First, the sample letter:

From: Terence Schiller MD
[Address and phone number included in the original.]

Date: 3/25/2017

To: President Donald Trump
The White House
1600 Pennsylvania Ave, NW
Washington, DC 20500

Subject: A plan inspired by the fifty thousand unnecessary deaths occurring per year in the United States due to prescription- and street-drug abuse.

Dear President Trump:

I have written this letter to all of the senators on the health committee and to President Obama in the preceding administration and gotten no response.

I am writing to you on behalf of the more than fifty thousand people each year who die from overdoses of prescription medicine and street drugs. This is a greater loss per year than those suffered in any of our recent wars. Now 1.5 times as many people die from drug abuse than die in car accidents. In 2017 the death rate from drug abuse *surpassed* the death rate of sixty-eight thousand per year that prevailed during WWII. Soon we will have homemade W-18, W-15, and 3-methylfentanyl drugs on the streets, which I suspect may increase the death toll to one hundred thousand young people a year. This is World War III, and we are losing.

It's vital to understand that the death toll *does not stem from just heroin from Mexico*. More than half of the deaths are the result of the abuse of US-made prescription medicine. When we suppress sales of one drug, there is an increase in the sales of others. So if we stop all illegal heroin imports, the abuse of US-made narcotics will still replace them. The "wall" alone will not help without other controls imposed on the entire drug-abuse industry. More people die from the abuse of oxycodone than street heroin, and oxycodone is made in the United States. Even If we stop all illegal imports of street drugs, homemade fentanyl will replace them. Fentanyl is more dangerous, and the death toll will increase.

Today, dangerous addictive drugs are more available to young people than ever before. Doctors are being pressured more to use them, see line item-4. Their street value is at a record high. The dissemination and misuse of these drugs is resulting in an epidemic of death in our young people. Frequently, the use of these medications results from legitimate needs. People have injuries or back pain, and so the medications are prescribed to them. The anxiety that people feel in stressful situations in their lives is made more tolerable by the use of anxiety medications. Unfortunately the medications can be extremely addictive, and patients pursue further prescription renewals. Friends and family members may be invited to use medications that were not prescribed for them. Some patients learn that they can sell these medications for large amounts of money. Many users move on to heroin use. And so a nationwide problem has been born.

There are countless articles written now in newspapers, magazines, and national television programs about the abuse of narcotics and benzodiazepine medications; it is now common knowledge. Working as a doctor I see the signs of abuse countless times. I see frequent hospital admissions of persons who are addicted to these medications. I've personally lost two patients who went doctor shopping to obtain multiple prescriptions for the same medications and accidentally killed themselves with them.

Many states are recognizing this problem and are taking excellent steps to reduce it. The state of New Jersey has an excellent program by which doctors can evaluate a patient's record to see if the patient has already obtained dangerous prescriptions. The doctor simply signs onto the Internet on a secure site and checks previous prescriptions that patients have received, see line item-1. This prevents a doctor from accidentally overprescribing or duplicate prescribing these medications. Since New Jersey and other states have initiated this program, I noticed almost immediately that patients started going from state to state to obtain prescriptions. Their ability to obtain drugs across state lines reduces the efficacy and safety of the program. Also, doctors are not required to utilize this program; in fact, most of them are unaware of it and not utilizing it. Hospitals are not required to utilize this program. It is simply not enforced or automatic. "Automatic" is what we should strive for.

The state of New York has recognized a massive problem, as I have. They have now initiated a new program by which no state hospital can provide more than three days of pain-medicine prescriptions to an emergency-room patient. This allows patients to obtain immediate, necessary pain control and gives them some time to get to their family doctors, who know the patients better. The program helps prevent the abuse of emergency-room visits just to get prescriptions for opioids.

I know you are incredibly busy. I also know you will be the president who listens to the people, understands the problems that they have, and solves those problems. Mr. President, please let me help you solve this problem. I have enclosed my multistep plan for eliminating unnecessary deaths by drug abuse. In an effort to keep this letter short, I will just tell you that this problem can be solved on a national basis without the need for any new taxes and without any compromise of patient care.

To date, efforts to stop this drug-abuse war are *not centrally guided* or *nationally based*. Current efforts consist of what I consider *misguided cellular research* by the NIDA. The counterproductive release of data to schoolchildren by the NIDA

- Does not address the gateway drugs.
- Encourages the free dissemination of how to make the drugs.
- Does not empower health-care professionals to stop drug abuse.
- Does not empower law enforcement enough.
- Does not collect proper data to monitor the problem.
- Does not control social media, which is encouraging drug abuse.
- Does not require news media to report on the problem to educate our citizens.
- Does not inform the public of the presence of drug dealers in the community, nor does it protect our schools and schoolchildren enough.
- Does not even suggest any long-term plan.

I have a plan to do all these things. I have a plan to win this war. Following are the basic steps of my plan. It uses automatic *engineering barriers* to substance abuse and pill mills, rather than unenforceable legislation.

I would, of course, provide my undivided attention to this problem and I'm available to travel and coordinate efforts because of my strong belief in this project. Please don't hesitate to telephone me twenty-four hours a day, 365 days a year. My cell number is [provided in original].

The misuse of these prescription medicines is now its own problem, together with the availability of new gateway-to-street drugs like heroin fentanyl, W-18, and W-15.

Sincerely,
Terence G. Schiller, MD

● ● ●

Here is the plan I have been mailing out and receiving no response.

Introduction: Numbers Define the Problem
(and numbers are increasing all the time)

I have only included the data that I found from highly trusted sources, so not all years are included. And up-to-date, recent data are always hard to find. Each of the numbers from previous years can be considered greatly increased for our current times.

One way to define the problem of substance abuse in America is to look at the numbers in terms of cost in dollars and cost in terms of lives lost and lives injured. We can compare these numbers to other problems that have these costs, such as wars.

Hospital visits involve cost. Forty-two percent of ER visits are just for prescription-drug abuse. (Abuse of street drugs only accounts for 20 percent of ER visits.)

For oxycodone alone: In 2009, we had 65,146 emergency-room visits. In 2011, we had 160,398. The United States contains 5 percent of the world population but consumes 81 percent of the world's oxycodone. Per recent government data, one in thirty high-school students abuses oxycodone; 1,442,000 abused oxycodone last year; 6,973,000 have abused it at some point in their lives. All this data is constantly changing, so I invite you to do your own up-to-date research.

For benzodiazepine—prescription antianxiety medicine—alone: in 2011, we had 103,653 ER visits at an average cost of $1,233 to $2,128 per visit.

In terms of lives: in 2014, 47,055 deaths occurred from drug abuse. This figure equates to a school bus of forty-seven children all getting killed every 8.75 hours all year long. Pharmaceutical drug deaths outnumber heroin deaths: 18,893 versus 10,574, in 2014. In 2016, we passed fifty thousand lives lost. In 2017, more than sixty thousand lives were lost. As a result of drug abuse, One and a half times more people die each year than those who die in auto accidents.

Compared to war:

- In each year of the Iraq War, 722 troops died (4,333 total).
- In each year of the Vietnam War, 2,911 died (58,200 total).
- In each year of World War II, 69,800 died (418,800 total).

In the 2016 *drug war*, more than fifty thousand died, which set a new record. Since 2000 we have lost about five hundred thousand to substance abuse— more American lives lost than in World War II. Every single year we lose about as many young people as we did in the entire twenty-year-long Vietnam War. And young people are dying at more than *sixty* times the rate of death in the Iraq War.

TOTAL DOLLARS

Calculating this takes a long time and tons of research. One government study of the total cost of drug abuse to society for 2007 took until 2011 to publish. It included health care, criminal justice, and workplace costs, and reported a cost of $55.7 billion. For 2008 I have found the statistic of 26,608 drug deaths. Today we have surpassed that number annually. So cost to current society could be well over $100,000 billion. And this does not include direct government spending on and by agencies to study and combat drugs. That probably adds another $25 billion.

The 2007 study seems to have left out what I call caregiver cost—for example, the need of a wife to apply for welfare for herself and children when the breadwinner husband dies of a drug overdose. Another study by the National Drug Intelligence Center(The Economic Impact of Illicit Drug Use on American Society" estimated a cost of $183 billion for 2007.

The Drug-Abuse Death-Reduction Plan Summary

Plan Mission Statement

The plan seeks to reduce currently high death rates (more than sixty thousand deaths per year) from overuse, misuse, and secondary sale of prescription painkillers and anxiety medication that lead to use of street drugs.

Deaths from abuse of prescription drugs outnumber deaths from heroin by two to one. The plan is needed because the use of prescription pain medicine is not only its own problem but also the gateway to the use of street drugs. This plan employs impenetrable engineering barriers against the practices of pill-mill doctors and the sale of prescription meds on the streets.

Summary of Plan Elements

The plan shall

- provide prescribers with a database of information on their patients' existing prescriptions for these medications. The availability of such a database can prevent prescribers from exceeding known efficacy limits for the doses of these medications and close down pill-mill doctors;
- utilize the existing core measure system to incentivize and enforce proper surveillance of dangerous prescriptions;
- dissuade performance-scoring systems that otherwise would empower patients over prescribers to misuse these medications;
- provide a vehicle to remove unused medications from circulation;
- empower law enforcement to remove drug sellers from business without having to actually witness the deals they make; and
- reduce childhood exposure to gateway drugs.

Details of plan elements are provided in the appendix. Here I try to give only the basic concept of each aspect of the national plan, to allow for faster reading. This format also reflects my development process. Over the years, I, along with those who provided input, have selected ideas and then refined them in more detail.

Plan Elements (39)

1. National database of drugs of misuse, including narcotics, benzo-diazepine, and others, for health-care providers to access and avoid duplicating prescriptions. This is currently modeled by the New Jersey program.

   We would sell advertising on this database website to fund the program. Use of this system would be neither optional nor mandatory but simply automatic: *every time* a doctor enters a pre-scription, the system would interrogate the patient's history and the doctor's history (see information on the "PMIX system" in Appendix-1.)

2. Ceiling-dose effect: monthly prescription limits that providers would not be permitted to exceed. This is the *most opposed* aspect of this plan; it is already being considered by some agencies and already under attack by patients and doctors who don't want their doses limited. Exceptions can be made for hospice patients and cancer patients. Honest patients would get the medicine they need, and patients who don't demonstrate a need for high doses will be limited to a proven safe level of dosing (see A-2).

3. New core measures that would provide doctors with no other recourse but to check the national database prior to writing prescriptions for the target medications. The database system would have a lockout feature. If the doctor does not log into the system to check, the phar-macy cannot fill the script without the pharmacist checking first. This would apply to both inpatient and outpatient contexts (see A-3).

4. Changes to all patient-satisfaction scoring systems to remove all chronic-pain and anxiety patients from these systems. Development of core criteria to define chronic-pain patients will be done by me (see A-4).

5. Pharmacy "call back–take back" programs: depositories for unused medications with dangerous misuse potential. These programs would run not just periodically but every day (see A-5).

6. National data collection for cause of death, with a boxed entry on the death certificate stating, "Death is substance related" and asking the signer to indicate yes or no; if yes, select the substance from a list and note whether it was prescribed or obtained by other means. This system will be used to track more accurate cause of death for drug users and allow us to learn exactly where people are dying and why. This information will be used to continuously improve the program.

7. Use of a single printer or 100 percent use of Escribe and a true watermark on paper prescriptions, to prevent counterfeit scripts. A single script can be worth $7,200 and is easier to counterfeit than a twenty-dollar bill. These prevention measures are already being taken in some states, but, again, the effort needs to be national. All paper scripts would still need Escribing verification in the national database. A single printer reduces surveillance personnel cost.

8. Fine and penalty system for patients who distribute or sell prescription medicine and the persons who buy or accept them. This is difficult to detect and enforce in many but not all cases.

9. Loss of license for offending doctors. I have seen doctors get caught selling narcotic prescriptions and then go on to do it again. We need a zero-tolerance system: if you're caught once, you're out.

10. Reorganization of the NIDA into a fighting team against drug abuse. Rename it the Task Force against Drug Abuse. Stop useless research and start doing something constructive (see A-10).

11. Mandatory textbooks about drug abuse in K–16 as well as military service, but *not* the terrible literature printed by the NIDA. An example of this existing literature is seen in the section on remodeling the NIDA. I will write these books and explain all the dangers of these drugs.

12. Mandatory news reporting of drug deaths every day. These would simply be public safety messages and can be made mandatory

using existing systems. People need to know how big a problem drug abuse is.

13. No new tax system for funding the program. The NIDA has a budget of more than one billion dollars a year, with no results of lowering the overdose rate to show for it. Stop this waste of money, and apply it where it will do more good.

14. Monitoring and feedback processes to vet the efficacy of the system. Item 6 is a big part of this to collect more detailed data on which drug caused the overdose and to achieve an organized effort to continue researching sources of the drugs and psychosocial aspects of their users. This is what the NIDA and other government agencies should be doing, under one leadership. Each aspect of this system will need an efficacy measure. I could easily develop these measures.

15. Clear-cut laws regulating the transport of medications outside the house, through the use of my "carry law." Existing carry laws are not well written nor clearly defined (see the Carry Law section following item 39 in this list.)

    Items 16, 17, 18, 19 are all related and build on each other. The system underlying these four items is the same as existing child-pornography laws, which constitute, therefore, a full precedent for my laws on abusing and tampering with drugs. This is a difficult section to understand; please read the appendix carefully. We can control the use of social media in distributing drugs and information about how to abuse drugs the same way we control child pornography.

16. Tampering with a medicine (e.g., crushing it) is to be considered an offense (see A-16).

17. Teaching another person how to tamper with or abuse a medicine is to be considered an offense (see A-17).

18. Aiding or teaching another person how to tamper with or abuse a medicine with the use of Internet video, text, print, social media, or mail is to be punishable also at a higher level (see A-18).

19. All social media and print media shall screen 100 percent of its entries for signs of encouraging substance abuse and censor any

entries that encourage it. Presenting instructions on breaking the law is breaking the law.

20. Taxes levied on any industry resisting these proposed changes, in the amount it would take to pay government to do what the industry is resisting. Law enforcement can be brought in to carry this out, as it is in the cases of child abuse and child pornography.

21. Development of a way for the Centers for Medicare and Medicaid Services (CMS) not to pay pill-mill doctors. Do not allow hybrid (cash-plus-Medicaid) practices or billing. The CMS does not lack for ways to deny payment to legitimate doctors. So the CMS can apply ways to deny payment to doctors who contribute to substance abuse (see A-21).

22. Megan's Law for drug dealers. If someone abuses one child, he or she is labeled publicly for life. But dealers can kill hundreds with drugs, and no one finds out about them. Change in this area must be implemented very carefully to prevent further abuse. Please see the details in A-22.

23. A gateway-drug law. The concept of the gateway drug is well established. Any substance that a young person uses to feel better can be a gateway to the use of stronger drugs. The NIH has established what the community has always known—that nicotine is a gateway drug. Alcohol is also known to be a gateway drug. Our children should not be exposed to advertising for these substances without parental guidance. We need a law prohibiting the advertising of these substances within the viewing range of schools and school-bus stops and children. During the time I have taken to research and write this book, new laws regarding tobacco advertising have come about. We need to push the concepts embodied in these laws further to include alcohol and marijuana, to stop exposing our children to advertising to substances that have been shown to be gateway substances (see A-23).

24. Patent law. Drug dealers have started making their own drugs; they learn how to by reading drug patents, which are online and

in the public domain. This has to be stopped; there is no need for these manufacturing processes to be public information—made so by the government (see A-24).

25. The increase of school drug-free zones to one mile or more based on local information to include all children who walk to school and the addition of quadruple-damages clauses to all drug laws (like the triple-damages clauses that apply to nursing homes; see A-25).

26. Analog law. We need a national drug analog law prohibiting the production of analogs, which would otherwise escape law enforcement. We currently have fifty analog laws, and none of them is clear or binding enough to do the job (see A-26). I have examples there that illustrate how, given the way current laws are written, they can be rendered unenforceable. My version of an analog law will do the job. I will write it with legal help.

27. Patch-for-patch law. Containerized pain medicine like patches, sprays, and pops can still be abused when they are done. Some counties require return of the spent patches to obtain new patches. This has reduced crime and saved lives, so it needs to be national— not just patch-for-patch but all media for all media.

28. Implementation of a monthly patient-condition monitoring system for all patients above 50 percent of the ceiling-dose limit. This would be just like the existing system for the medicine clozaril (see, Appendix, A-28).

29. Implementation of a "pay for performance" system that will lower reimbursement for doctors or hospitals if their patients suffer from an overdose. This would be just like several existing systems (see A-29).

30. A revised national "prescription defense" law that includes expiration dating for prescriptions. The law will provide tiered levels of expiration dates applicable to the "defense" of carrying pills in your pocket. States may raise levels but not lower them (see A-30).

31. A ceiling on the number of prescriptions that any one doctor, nurse practitioner, or advanced-practice nurse may write in a day. We have seen a single doctor write 423 scripts per day for a total of 110,012 per year (i.e., one script every one minute, twenty-five seconds) for a total of 12.3 million pills (see A-31).

32. Maximized research and development of nonnarcotic pain-control medicine and nonbenzo anxiety medicine and the funding of research only for nonsedating pain meds. This system would resemble what the government already does in many other industries. But big pharmaceutical companies seem to be left uncontrolled (see A-32).

33. Required use of, and third-party payment of, nonnarcotic pain medicine and modalities both in hospitals and other outpatient services. Insurance companies would not be permitted to deny payment for proven treatments that are alternatives to narcotics (see A-33).

34. Mandatory drug-weaning plans. Frequently, a person is started on strong narcotic pain medicine for good reasons, and then later his or her doctor tries to stop its continued use. If the dose is high, a person may experience withdrawal symptoms. These unpleasant symptoms can prompt patients to restart medicines that they may not need anymore. For this reason, every time doctors prescribe pain medicines, they need to also provide weaning or tapering instructions. Many such instructions are available, and I could easily produce a booklet of instructions for doctors and patients to access. All insurance carriers would be required to pay for the weaning medication if additional pills are required. And doctors and hospitals would have to provide free visits to uninsured patients with weaning questions or problems. Insurance companies must cover drug-weaning visits up to a limit.

35. Control of the partial pain-management practice. There are many well-meaning doctors—and some not so well-meaning—who still will have a few patients receiving narcotics that are destined for

abuse. We have nine hundred thousand doctors, so if half of them have a few patients who obtain even a reasonable number of pills that are distributed for recreation, this will be a large problem that may escape detection. At this writing I am reserving my plans for this. It is difficult to detect this behavior by doctors or patients. But the other provisions in this plan will greatly reduce drug diversion from its present level. Stay tuned for more.

36. Anti–doctor-shopping laws. I have already mentioned how persons go from doctor to doctor and state to state to obtain prescriptions for narcotics, thereby obtaining lots of pills to abuse or sell. Every state has—and nationally we have—some form of law against this. But I am willing to bet that no person has ever been put in jail for this. Do you really think a doctor is going to press charges against a patient for getting pain pills from multiple doctors?

    This doctor shopping happens every day, and it's a large, well-known problem in the medical community. Now take another look at items 1 and 2. Do you see how we have replaced an absolutely unenforceable administrative law with an engineering roadblock to criminal activity? Any would-be patient could go to any number of doctors but will still be limited to a ceiling dose. No law enforcement would be required and no cost to impose on taxpayers. Even if my system is implemented, there will still be people trying to doctor-shop to obtain more pills. See the next item to learn how we will again set up an engineering roadblock against even attempting to doctor shop—again, at no cost to the taxpayer (see A-36).

37. Doctor and pharmacy lock-in laws. Your medical-insurance company only lets you go to some doctors. You can select among those, but if you then go to a different doctor, the visit is not paid for. If you try to use a credit card at a store that doesn't accept it, it will not work. But you can still go to as many doctors as you want and to as many pharmacies as you want and pay cash and get enough narcotic pills to sell on the street or just get addicted to. Again, we

see controls on corporate (i.e., insurance-company) money spent but none on your safety.

We can impose such control with our engineering roadblock of monthly dosage limits, but we can even do better. We can stop even an attempt to get extra pills. Many states do this now, and so do some countries. By locking a patient into only one doctor and pharmacy, the patient can't even attempt to obtain excess pills from other doctors.

Lock-ins would occur only for controlled drugs. You could still go to urgent cares, ERs, or any other doctor or pharmacy for everything else. So, if you didn't take narcotics or antianxiety meds, you would never even know the system existed. And if you go to a pain doctor and only use one pharmacy, again, nothing changes for you. States provide an allowance of a seventy-two-hour emergency supply of meds if needed—for example, if you get hurt away from home. All in all, it would be a very nice way to obtain great control with no inconvenience except to persons trying to get lots of pills to sell or doctors trying to run a pill mill. But again, this must be a national effort, as persons still can go to different states and have many doctors and pharmacies to support their pill-selling business.

38. Overdose discharge planning. If you needed a lifesaving medicine and a hospital discharged you without it, what would you think of the hospital? How about if the hospital discharged a dementia patient with ten pages of discharge instructions to read—what would you think? Suppose you became diabetic and they gave you prescriptions for insulin, needles, and a glucometer machine and told you to figure out how to use them when you get them, and it's Saturday night and your pharmacy is closed. Or suppose you were taken to the ER after you had a life-threatening allergic reaction to eating a peanut, and they discharged you and said, "Don't eat peanuts ever again." Everyone knows peanut oil is in many things and is not 100 percent avoidable, so the doctor should give you

a prescription for an EpiPen to inject yourself with if it happens again. It all sounds stupid, doesn't it? Well, I'm sorry to say, this stuff happens all the time.

Each illness needs a specific set of discharge medicine, equipment, scheduled follow-up appointments, and attention to patients, to make sure they understand what they must do and how to do it. Then, if patients have no insurance or not enough money to pay for what's needed—a terrible problem—social workers step in to do their very tough and important job of helping. Any hospital doctor knows that the discharge of a patient requires a lot of work to make sure everything is planned for.

Discharging overdose patients is harder than most other cases. Many don't have insurance. Some have no home or were kicked out of a good home for doing drugs. Then there is the technical part of the drug they used. How long will the sedative effect of the drug last? Are there effects lingering hours, days, and even weeks later? When is it safe to discharge such patients and to where and with what instructions? Many overdose patients die hours after they have been discharged. See A-38 on this issue and how to save these lives, too.

39. Stopping off-label use of narcotics. When a doctor gives you a medicine, you understand that the medicine has been studied and is designed to help you with your particular problem. If you have a strep throat, the doctor will give you amoxicillin to kill the bacteria, and you will feel better. The doctor has studies to prove that he is giving you the correct medicine. Sometimes a doctor will use a medicine that has not been studied for a particular condition, but there is a strong compelling reason for the doctor to try it.

I'm sorry to say that sometimes doctors go too far and use medicines very inappropriately. Worse than that, sometimes the pharmaceutical industry also goes too far and actually market medicines to doctors inappropriately, leading to dangerous prescriptions given to unsuspecting patients. Patients may become hurt or even die or survive but remain addicted to the medicines.

In the engineering industry, we used to say that some safety regulations are written in blood. In other words, people had to die before a new rule was made to improve safety. In engineering we usually can see a problem. In medicine a problem is usually unseen, not obvious. This means that lawmakers would never be able to prevent a medical/health problem. Only an experienced doctor or other medical professional could anticipate some problems. Allowing doctors to use narcotics and benzodiazepine medicine for illnesses that the drugs were not studied for is a deadly, addiction-inducing practice.

A surefire way to get a person addicted to a medicine for pain is to use a medicine that does not completely control the pain. It will cause the patient to want more, unless the patient is made very aware that the medicine will only relieve some of the pain regardless of the dose. The use of less-than-adequate medicines is a practice that our lawmakers need to understand especially regarding the ceiling doses and need for better safer medicine. I do understand this, and you will too, I hope, after reading this.

The use of off-label narcotics has become so pervasive and so dangerous that persons are getting addicted to drugs and dying from them. And yes, some pharmaceutical companies are literally pushing doctors to use these medicine on anyone, regardless of the drugs' efficacy, and are sometimes getting paid, reportedly, as much as $9,000 for a one-month prescription. Company executives have even reached the point of being arrested for misleading doctors to write prescriptions for off-label use of narcotics. Again, only when people started to die did the government take action. In my plan, the problem does not even have a chance to start let alone prove fatal.

This is a very important section, because allowing doctors to write prescriptions for off-label use of narcotics would allow a sort of escape from the national prescription-monitoring system and restart pill-mill-like practices again. Put another way, it would be a sort of technical loophole that would lead to getting people hooked on drugs again.

It is also very difficult for me to explain this issue in terms that a nondoctor would understand. If you only see two points here, I urge you to understand that some pharmaceutical company executives will push drugs to the point of actually being arrested after patients died from their actions and that doctors can succumb to financial bribes and greed. My plan for curtailing off-label use of narcotics will stop these shady dealings and still allow patients who would benefit from the drugs to get them simply by doctors following the already written indications for these medicines. Please see A-39.

• • •

The Carry Law

Background

In order to arrest a person for selling or dealing prescription narcotics, a law officer must actually witness the deal go down, with money exchanged for drugs. It is extremely rare to get close enough to witness this. The final distribution of drugs to users is done all over the country in public places at night, in the dark, behind doors, or otherwise out of sight. Law enforcement needs a way to control distributors of drugs without having to see deals take place.

We cannot charge a person with selling drugs without proof, but we can control the drug distribution with a law that will impact sales. We need a truly national pill-carrying law.

The Logic behind the Law

Scheduled drugs are dangerous and need to be controlled. Presently we have no real controls on them. You can put a bottle of narcotic pills in your pocket and take them to a nightclub or bar and be protected by law, when we all know that there is often no reason to do so unless you plan on giving them away or selling them. If you need to take a pill with you for real reasons that too can be handled in my carry law. Can we control this behavior and still not interfere with a doctor-patient relationship? Yes, we can; please read on. This law will provide for the control of persons who distribute controlled substances for sale without keeping these substances away from those who need them.

The Law

Definitions: short-acting drugs (SADs)—those whose effect on pain lasts for less than eight hours; long-acting drugs (LADs)—those whose effect on pain lasts for twelve hours.

1. LADs are not allowed outside the house.
2. Patient has one hour to get them home from the pharmacy.
3. If caught with a bottle en route from the pharmacy, the bottle must be full, as none is to be taken before getting the bottle home.
4. Police have the right to analyze all pills to see if they are real.
5. The prescription date and time is stamped with a tamper-proof seal on the bottle, like the seal on cigarettes.
6. Police are permitted access to pharmacy records to confirm the validity of a prescription.
7. SADs must be accompanied with a doctor's script on how they are used and how many the patient is allowed to take out of the house for a day at work, which should be no more than three pills (for eighteen hours). A new script every month is required.
8. A doctor's script for meds during travel is required.
9. SADs or LADs are not permitted in school at all, especially K–16.

10. If medically needed a doctor's script for meds brought to college or any other school should specifically mention the school.
11. Users must register their home address in the national computer system.
12. No meds are allowed outside the prescription bottle or in any other container—that is, bottle to mouth only is permissible.
13. A pharmacy must provide a carry bottle or blister pack to a patient needing an SAD outside the house. This bottle is to be renewed monthly with date and time stamped and "one-day quantity" printed on it. So patients who must take pills to work will get two bottles: one with the month's supply, to leave at home, and another as described here, to carry.

    Patients on unemployment or disability do not get carry bottles.
14. There is to be no mailing of pills or scripts at all.

Who would be offenders of this law?

- Anyone with a pill in his or her pocket
- Anyone with pills in nonpharmacy containers, even at home, with the exception of a pill organizer
- Anyone with more than three pills in a carry bottle outside the house
- Anyone carrying any LAD that is not a full bottle with a seal intact and being transported between the pharmacy and home, or that does not meet carry-bottle requirements

APPENDIX

With detailed explanations of selected line items of the Drug-Abuse
Death Reduction Program

• • •

A-1   National database of drugs of misuse

A-2   Ceiling-dose effect

A-3   New core measures

A-4   Changes to all patient-satisfaction-scoring systems

A-5   Pharmacy "call back–take back" programs

A-10 Reorganization of the NIDA

A-16 Tampering with a medicine law

A-17 Teaching another person how to tamper with law

A-18 Aiding or teaching another person how to tamper with or abuse a medicine with the use of Internet video, text, print, social media, or mail law

A-21 Development of a way for the Centers for Medicare and Medicaid Services (CMS) not to pay pill-mill doctors

A-22 Megan's Law for drug dealers

A-23 A gateway-drug law

A-24 Patent law

A-25 The increase of school drug-free zones to one mile

A-26 Analog law

A-28 Implementation of a monthly patient-condition monitoring system

A-29 Implementation of a "pay for performance" system

A-30 A revised national prescription defense law

A-31 A ceiling on the number of prescriptions that any one doctor, nurse practitioner, or advanced-practice nurse may write in a day

A-32 Maximized research and development of nonnarcotic pain-control medicine and nonbenzo anxiety medicine

A-33 Required use of, and third-party payment of, nonnarcotic pain medicine and modalities both in hospitals and other outpatient services

A-36 Anti–doctor-shopping laws

A-38 Overdose discharge planning

A-39 Stopping off-label use of narcotics

A-1
Discussion of the proposed national database of drugs of misuse

It's well understood that persons seeking to abuse or sell prescription painkillers can go to many doctors to obtain multiple prescriptions. I find examples of this when I use the New Jersey Prescription Monitoring (NJPMP) system in my medical practice. Persons now travel from state to state to obtain multiple prescriptions for narcotics to sell. The pills typically are up to eighty milligrams in dosage and sell for a dollar per milligram.

States have prescription-monitoring programs, but they do not contribute to a national database. So persons can go to several states and even fly to faraway states to obtain more pills. And this practice encourages the pill-mill doctor's office, in which a doctor will write large prescriptions in return for cash-paying patients.

Pill mills are well-known entities that have even been the subject of television programs. Many government agencies have studied this phenomenon but have never followed through with a definitive plan to stop it. We will.

I don't understand why we continue to monitor only on a state level. Some states do coordinate and share data about sellers and doctors, but without a true national program, persons seeking to make a business out of selling prescription drugs will simply change their travel patterns to find cooperative doctors in other states. Besides, there is no enforcement upon doctors to check any prescription-monitoring system prior to giving out prescriptions.

The Substance Abuse and Mental Health Services Association has studied integrating EScribe with monitoring programs, and it found great benefit back in 2012, but no follow-through has taken place.

The American Association for Automation in Pharmacy also continues to struggle in its attempts to bring automated monitoring to reality.

The National Association of State-Controlled Substance Authorities continues to try to improve monitoring programs, along with the Academy of Pain Management, the National Alliance for Model State Drug Laws, and the National Association of Boards of Pharmacy.

Everyone seems to know that we need a national, automated prescription-monitoring program except our national government and the National Institute on Drug Abuse.

Doctors need an automatic and mandatory drug-usage system to include the following information:

- Questionable-activity reports
- Unsolicited-usage reports
- Near-ceiling-dose reports
- At-ceiling-dose reports

We now have a Prescription Drug Monitoring Program Training and Technical Assistance Center (http://www.pdmpassist.org/; 781-609-7741) funded at Brandeis University. They help with two hubs. The one in Boston is called RxCheck, with ten states using its PMIX computer architecture. The other uses PMP InterConnect, with thirty-five states funded under the Bureau of Justice Assistance's Harold Rogers PDMP (Prescription Drug Monitoring Program) grants.

In 2018 we will pass a major milestone; we will begin to lose the lives of more young Americans each year than we did in World War II (68,000 per year). Our previous president pardoned more than one thousand drug offenders, letting them back on the street because they did "nonviolent crimes." Many were drug dealers according to articles published in papers such as the *Chicago Tribune*. A list of the drug dealers pardoned can be found in a Department of Justice report available on that website. I guess Obama felt that killing people with narcotics is not violent.

More than half of American deaths are from prescription drugs, and most heroin addicts started with prescription drugs. When addicts don't have access to heroin, they will seek out prescription drugs like fentanyl and oxycodone.

America needs a national program that is mandatory and automatic so that no person can go doctor shopping to collect drugs and sell them on the street or abuse them. I will show you how to build this program. As explained above, it is started for us in most states, and we have people who can run it. Reorganizing the NIDA will help pay for it.

Let me explain how the system works now. In New Jersey, when I write a prescription for a narcotic, I can check the NJPMP system online and obtain a report showing what medicines the patient has had in the past year, which doctors prescribed them, and which pharmacies filled it. This sounds good, but it has problems and is not national. For one thing, the system is too slow. It takes as long as forty days for a script to show up in the database. Using the database is considered mandatory, but there is no way to enforce that, and most doctors don't use it. Nearly every day in the office, I find a report of multiple doctors prescribing the same narcotic to one patient. Sometimes the reports are very bad, with the patient getting narcotics from multiple doctors on the same day—easy to do, because NJPMP is not a real-time system. You could doctor shop for thirty days before your activities would show up. Or you could just pick multiple states that are not online with each other and travel to them to get more pills to sell, give away, or abuse.

If computer systems could be linked, producing a national database, such traveling would stop. Then the system would have to be linked to electronic prescribing so that doctors would have to use it to generate scripts. At that point, there would be no worry about the cost involved in enforcing its use; the doctor would simply use the computer to generate a prescription in real time, without the forty-day delay. Doctors will be limited in the number of prescriptions they can write in a day, and patients will be limited to ceiling doses.

Doctors would also be able to retrieve from the system and see reports about their patients, such as the following:

- Questionable-activity reports. These would show that although the patient hit a ceiling-dose limit, he or she continued to attempt to have other doctors prescribe more medicine, indicating that this patient is doctor shopping.
- Unsolicited usage reports. These would be reports, for example, of patients obtaining pills from other local doctors and/or out of state. They would be e-mailed to the patients' main doctors, alerting them that certain patients may need visits to discuss why such activities occurred. Are their pains getting worse, or are they trying to obtain pills for recreation or sale? Do they need other forms of pain management?
- Near-ceiling-dose-limit reports. When a patient obtains enough pills to be at this level of dosage, the doctor(s) involved would be alerted.
- At-ceiling-dose-limit reports. When a patient has reached his or her maximum dose limit, the doctor(s) involved would be alerted.

But at present, Amazon, eBay, and your credit-card company likely have more comprehensive computer systems than your doctor has.

A national, automatic computer system to control medications as appropriate for the level of danger that they have brought to bear on our country: how could anyone possibly disagree with this need?

A-2
Discussion of the ceiling-dose effect

To fully understand the issue at hand, let's look at a patient whom I once met. This is the worst example of the issue that I have ever seen, though I have known of hundreds of other, less dramatic, cases.

I was an internist in a major city hospital, and I was called to consult on a young woman who was to get multiple surgeries. She needed surgery to close wounds on her heels and sacrum. She also had wounds over her shoulder blades and on the back of her head. The sacral wound was very deep and large; it would need a muscle flap and skin flap to close it. This is a common wound on paralyzed patients. They can't move, so they lie in bed motionless and get bedsores or bed wounds as constant pressure on parts of the body destroys skin, fat, and muscle—even bone.

I spoke with her at length. She related a story of being in a car accident, followed by surgery, pain, and now the wounds. I asked, "Was this the accident that left you paralyzed?"

She answered, "I'm not paralyzed."

"Well, I mean, that left you unable to walk?"

"I can walk fine."

Now I was confused. So I just asked, "Then why do you have these wounds?"

She replied, "Because I lie in bed all day. I get up, eat, take my pills, go back to bed in the morning, and then do it again in the evening. I'm in bed all the time. So I got bedsores."

I was still confused. Why was she in bed all day? I continued to collect the medical history that I would need to care for her. I asked what medicines she took, and she explained that she took sixteen hundred milligrams of OxyContin twice per day.

I quickly corrected her, saying, "You mean one hundred sixty milligrams."

"No, I take one thousand six hundred milligrams twice per day."

"Ma'am, that would be a handful of at least sixteen pills twice per day."

"Yes," she said, "that's how I take them." With this she cupped her hands together, held them to her mouth, and raised her hands as if to pour the pills into her mouth. "Then I fall asleep again."

I called the pharmacy, and they confirmed the dose and asked me, "Why so high a dose?"

You may already realize that 160 mg of Oxycontin is a very large dose; this patient had been worked up to ten times that dose, all prescribed not by a drug pusher but a doctor. And the side effect was nearly fatal.

I told her that I refused to give her that and that the pharmacy in the hospital would refuse also. She was OK with that and left it to me. In two days, I weaned her down to some five-milligram tablets about four times a day. And she was absolutely happy with that. I got her out of bed, and we developed a normal set of activities for her, with the help of physical therapy.

Apparently, the previous prescribing doctor would ask her if she had pain, and he would not stop escalating the dose until she said no. Again, it was clearly the worst offense of a ceiling-dose effect that I have ever seen. (I did contact a state medical association about this doctor.)

What is a ceiling-dose effect? Every medicine has a ceiling dose. This means that if you take more of the medicine, you get more effect, regardless of what it's for. So if you take more blood-pressure medicine, your pressure will go lower. Or if you take more of an antidepressant, you will be less depressed. But at some point, if the dose is too high, the side effects will hurt you and not give any better effect. That's when you have reached the ceiling-dose effect, what we often call the maximum dose of the medicine.

Everything in life has a ceiling dose—even water! If you use Benadryl, you know that a common dosage is 50 mg, but did you know that 7.5 g could kill you? The ceiling dose for water is thirty liters in one day for most people. If you drink more than thirty liters you will get symptoms—maybe even a coma—from it. Clearly there is a ceiling dose for opioids, because people die every day from prescription opioids. As we increase doses of a medicine, we start to see unwanted side effects. For opioids we see constipation early on. This is not a bad problem; we can avoid it by giving other medicine, even simple things like milk of magnesia, to reverse the constipation. But at higher doses, we start to see the dangers of somnolence and respiratory suppression. And in the case of the young woman, we see increasing doses causing reduced function. Even at lower doses than hers we start to see reduced functional capacity, such as trips and falls and increased reaction time. So there is a dosage that is high enough to give safe pain relief but not so high as to cause bad side effects.

You have paid millions of dollars in taxes for this issue to be studied, and by now the issue of dosage is well known. And as I have discussed under item 39, there are some types of pain for which opioids don't work well at all. There are several government-funded (i.e., you paid for them) studies showing two distinct levels at which side effects start to outweigh good effects, and an even higher level that one should almost never go above, as the side effects are very bad. Your government is spending large amounts of money to study a problem but doing nothing with the results.

Through a national computer system, we could follow patients, and when they get to 50 percent of ceiling dose, we could start to do lab tests to confirm that the patients are actually using the medicine themselves and not giving it to friends or selling it. This is already done by many pain clinics; it's not a new idea. We could follow the patients up to the ceiling dose and continue to confirm that they are using the medicine correctly and completely. Then, if the patient is still not satisfied, we can review what has been done to and/or for the patient to date—what procedures and what medicines—and look for better and safer ways to control the pain. Only at that point would we consider exceeding established ceiling-dose limits.

I have seen patients who were unsatisfied with pain control for, for example, a painful leg, even though they were seeing a pain doctor. When I evaluated them, I found that they had circulation problems. I referred them to an interventional radiologist, who opened blocked arteries in their legs, and their pains were completely removed without medicine. That is the proper way to follow patients who are nearing established ceiling limits. Don't just give them any dose; rather, reevaluate to look for unseen causes of pain.

Now, this is important: when you reach a ceiling dose and your pain is still not controlled, we need to look harder for ways to help you. That means your insurance company and Medicare cannot deny payment for pain-control diagnostics or intervention to a patient who is at ceiling dose. Again, I come back to the insurance companies and payers. They must pay for nonnarcotic pain control like prescription 8 percent Capsaicinpatches,

Transcutaneous electrical nerve stimulation units, surgery, chiropractic, physical therapy, and diagnostics such as expensive MRIs. If you are a significant-pain patient, you know what it's like to have a doctor's request to help you denied by an insurance company. You need power over the insurance companies, not power over the doctors. And a ceiling-dose-effect regulation should give you that power.

A-3
Discussion of new core measures

The Center for Medicare and Medicaid Services (CMS) and the Joint Commission on Accreditation of Health Care Organizations (JCAHO) have established points of measure to evaluate the quality of hospitals. Specific medical activities performed in the hospital are checked and can cause a hospital to suffer a reduction in reimbursement if they are not performed properly. For example, if an emergency-room patient was diagnosed with pneumonia, did the patient receive antibiotics within thirty minutes of diagnosis? If it took more than thirty minutes, then the hospital is not in compliance with the pneumonia core measure, and reimbursement could be reduced for all Medicare patients. This is an extremely powerful way to control the quality of work in hospitals. As a former chairman of medicine, I know exactly what effect these measures have.

There are about thirty of these measures, but none of them can stop hospitals or emergency rooms from duplicating prescriptions for narcotics. Persons have been known to go from ER to ER, shopping for drug prescriptions. Then they purchase multiple bottles of narcotics and sell them on the street. As a doctor working in five hospitals at once, I recall a man whom I discharged from one hospital. The next day, when I went to another hospital, I found him admitted under my name for the same illness, asking for pain medicine. I have seen other persons who shop ER to ER over many states. One such person didn't fool me only because a colleague who worked in ERs in Pennsylvania and New Jersey recognized her and notified me. Taxpayers are funding all these ER visits, of course.

So if a hospital takes more than thirty-one minutes to get an antibiotic to a patient, it loses money. But if it gives ninety OxyContin eighty-milligram pills to a patient who got ninety pills from another doctor three days earlier, CMS doesn't care. And our drug-pushing patient sells them for a dollar a milligram, earning $14,400 for three days work. Similar activity is now going on with the drugs used to treat withdrawal: neurontin and vistaril.

Here again, such activity could best be avoided using a national prescription-drug-monitoring database that is automatic and mandatory. However, until we build ours, the CMS can issue a core measure to require all ERs, hospitals, doctors, and pharmacies to check their state system before issuing any prescriptions for drugs of abuse. This would not cost the taxpayers a penny, and it would save lives. Why would anyone disagree with this?

We need this core measure *now*.

A-4
Discussion of changes to all patient-satisfaction scoring systems

Patients who enter an ER or are admitted to a hospital are now given an opportunity to score or rate their doctors and hospital on what are felt to be key measures of health care. They do this by filling out a patient survey, which is mailed to them after their visits. The main scoring system is the Hospital Consumer Assessment of Healthcare Providers and Systems (HCAHPS; pronounced "H caps"). One measure that they are scoring is pain control: "Did the doctor control your pain well?" And the consumer is asked to rate from "Always" (good) to "Never" (bad). The hospitals are penalized financially when they do not receive "always" ratings. I ask you, since when did doctors ever "always" relieve all pain all the time? Also, what does "control" mean? I can tell you that consumers think it means they will be 100 percent pain-free, which is impossible to achieve.

This survey system empowers consumers over doctors. And is creating danger for patients as seen in one study that has shown that hospitals with the best scores have the highest mortality.

I have seen patients come to the ER for repeat chronic problems, seeking narcotics. They will hold their paper surveys up in the air and say, "If you don't give me what I want, I will give you a bad survey." Good doctors who try to not overprescribe opioids have been fired from their jobs because they exercised appropriate caution with narcotic doses.

So we are left with so-called consumers accidentally killing themselves at a rate of fifty every nine hours. And these are the consumers who are asked to rate doctors or hospitals on how well they use opioids! The government invented this system.

We also see many chronic-pain patients who are already being treated by a doctor specializing in pain control. When these patients come to the ER because of an exacerbation of their pain, they are treated by internists or other ER doctors. What this amounts to is that chronic-pain patients whose pain is not controlled by their pain specialists are coming to emergency rooms and rating nonspecialty doctors for treating the pain. Would you have an ER doctor do open-heart surgery and then fire him if he is rated as having done a poor job? By virtue of the patients' pain being chronic, they are still going to have pain in the hospital, and their pain is not even *always* controlled when they are otherwise well.

I did my own research on many doctors in the hospital where I served as chairman of medicine. What I found is that doctors and nurses do a fantastic job of controlling all sorts of pain on narcotic-naïve patients in a hospital. But when patients have any recent use of alcohol, benzos, or narcotics, then control becomes very difficult and dangerous. Physiological changes have occurred in these patients; their situations are no longer doctor- or hospital-management problems.

We can have a pain-control survey, if needed, but practicing doctors must design it, not consumers. The medical profession is the only one that is rated officially by the government and penalized by people who wouldn't know how to do the job of doctors themselves.

The existing system is pushing doctors to *overprescribe* narcotics. I would put together a team of doctors, nurses, and pharmacists to redesign a survey system that would not do this. Instead, it would educate patients on how prescribing decisions are made, what to expect from pain control, and the understanding that their pain will not always be controlled. It would also be a system that does not include, or would make special provisions for, chronic-pain patients or patients already on narcotics.

A-5
Explanation of the pharmacy "call back–take back" programs

The DEA has already approved pharmacies to take back unused drugs and safely dispose of them—an example of the nice work the DEA does. To expand on this initiative, recall my idea of having doctors place expiration dates on narcotics prescriptions. They would help control the drugs better and reflect good medical practice generally.

Let me explain by an extreme example. I once met a man who came to the ER suffering from pneumonia. He had a badly broken leg and wore an external fixator with other metal orthopedic hardware. The fixator looked old, so I x-rayed the leg and found it to be completely healed. I offered to contact his orthopedic doctor to discuss removal of the hardware because he now had an infection—that is, pneumonia. He looked at me and said, "Oh, is it supposed to come off? It's two years old." He actually thought he needed it for life. He was not told that he needed to come back and have the device removed. We tell patients when to start a medicine, so it's only logical for us to tell them that by a given date they should be out of pain and no longer in need of the pills.

Now, if you break a bone and the doctor gives you some narcotic pain pills, that's fine. But if the pain is still there three weeks later, something is probably wrong, so it's good medicine to inform you that you should not need this pain medicine past two weeks (as an example). If the pain persists, you should come back to see the doctor again. If the pain is gone in a week and you have pills left over, good for you, but the remaining pills are dangerous to have around.

We all watched a young man sit at a table with President Trump and Chris Christie. The young man said on national TV, "I started my drug habit and addiction when I took some leftover OxyContin from my dad's medicine cabinet. It made me feel great, and I knew I always wanted to feel like that, so I was hooked."

The president replied, "I had no idea."

Well, I have an idea. Am I the only one who had a revelation from that young man? If you can't listen to a problem and think of a way to solve the problem, then why are you inviting the addict to the White House, to put on a show for the public? It's very clear to me. If the doctor who gave the pills to the dad had placed an expiration date on them, and the date was registered in a computer at the pharmacy, the dad could have received a recorded phone message from the pharmacy, advising him of the expiration date and asking him to bring unused pills back. It would work just like renting a video, or a tool from Home Depot—simple. Community take-back drop boxes are a good effort, but they are not nearly enough, not even for the wealthy, educated family of which the young man was a member. We need a system to alert us to bring the unused pills back. You have an alarm clock, don't you? Why not implement an alarm system like this, a concrete, proactive, computer-controlled plan to get dangerous pills back to a safe place not a year later but as soon as they are no longer needed? When the pharmacist fills a script, he or she enters the date into the computer, and the computer makes the calls, just as it does now, to tell you that you need a refill.

A-10
A discussion of the reorganization of the NIDA

The NIDA has done a great job of defining the opioid problem in terms of immediate effects and with data on drug abuse. But it has done nothing to prevent drug abuse except produce documents—just paper documents, no laws, no policies, no improvement. The problem has been increasing every year for decades. It's time to stop defining the problem and start solving it.

The NIDA has come closest to being proactive with a very bad attempt at creating written material that teachers can distribute to young people in the classroom. Actually, the material they have generated is indescribably inappropriate and likely contributes to the problem.

In a pamphlet on cocaine, the NIDA writes, "Cocaine is like chocolate or coffee...people feel an extra sense of pleasure." It has a "fascinating effect on the brain." The NIDA does mention that cocaine makes your heart beat harder, which it described as "like squeezing into a tight pair of pants." These are words of wisdom given to a fifth-grader: cocaine is like coffee and chocolate and has a fascinating effect on your brain, but it may make you feel like you are squeezing into a tight pair of pants. Does this sound like the message to give a young person about an illegal drug that kills thousands of people a year?

I have personally cared for cocaine overdoses in the ER and will always remember a young man who died of a massive intracranial hemorrhage in front of me while I was trying to get an IV line into him. I can tell you that he did not look like he was trying to get into a pair of tight pants. I have seen persons suffer a hemiplegic stroke after first using cocaine—their very first line. There are thirty-nine ways cocaine kills you, and none is mentioned by the NIDA pamphlet—not a single one!

In its opioid pamphlet, the NIDA makes no attempt to mention the dangers of these drugs at all! It explains that "opioids create pleasure, relaxation and contentment, and reduced pain, and stop cough." Are these authors out of their minds? Is this language that explains the danger of this medication to a schoolchild? The number-one killer prescription drug oxycodone was not mentioned. Of the nineteen ways that opioids kill you, none was mentioned—not a single one.

The NIDA has nine program initiatives. Stopping drug abuse is not one of them! Saving lives is not one of them. Let's reorganize this agency into the Task Force against Drug Abuse. Use my thirty-nine points. Have a single goal to stop drug deaths by reducing supply and demand for drugs and implementing the proper rehabilitation of users.

A-16, A-17, A-18

Discussion of laws against tampering with a medicine, teaching another person how to tamper, and aiding or teaching another person how to tamper with or abuse a medicine with the use of Internet video, text, print, social media, or mail

Many times, drug users will take drugs in manners different from those that are intended, in order to get high faster. They will chew pills that are supposed to be swallowed, or they will eat patches that were supposed to be placed on the skin. They will crush up a pill and snort it or put it in liquid and inject it. In an attempt to stop one such practice, a new pill has been developed that is very hard to crush. But people have quickly found ways to grind up the pills and snort them. This process is now available for any child to learn by watching YouTube videos.

Although difficult to monitor, tampering with medicine still needs to be illegal. Even if we never see it occur, it still needs to be illegal. The rationale for this seemingly futile law may be found in plan items 17, 18, and 19.

A-17

Discussion of Teaching of Tampering

It's clear that we do not want people grinding up narcotic pills to snort them. But it's also clear that we cannot enforce what people do behind closed doors in their houses. So the tampering law provides little to no protection or control on substance abuse. However, it does provide a foundation to control dissemination of information on how to abuse drugs. If tampering with a drug is illegal, then teaching a person how to tamper is also illegal, and this provides expansion to the tampering law. It also expands the number of persons responsible for substance abuse that may be prosecuted.

A-18
Discussion of Teaching Drug Abuse on Social Media

There are videos online about how to tamper with and abuse opana, exalgo, and OxyContin. There are videos on how to inject drugs. I saw a video about how to inject drugs that was produced by a needle-sales company. We all know that this material is leading to people dying, and fostering drug abuse, but we think we can't stop it because of freedom of speech. That's simply not true. We can outlaw these videos by building on items 16 and 17, just as we outlaw child pornography and for the same reasons. Read the following and see if the analogy is clear.

Child pornography is illegal, but adult pornography is not. Why? It's because we protect children until they can make their own choices and because making child-pornography videos involves molesting a child. And molesting a child is illegal. So the video is illegal. But wait, what if the video is made in a country that allows sex with children? If an American watches such a video, no crime is committed under US jurisdiction. So why do we still make the video illegal? It's because we know that people who watch such a video may go on to perform the acts in the video. So all child pornography videos are illegal in the United States. We must start with making child molestation illegal in order to make the videos illegal. Now, if someone made a video on how to entice a child into a car to molest the child, we would arrest that person. Let's simply apply the same logic and laws governing child abuse to substance abuse. Killing a child is also illegal, isn't it? Drug dealers kill more children than child molesters do—far more.

If tampering with a medicine is illegal, then anything related to it should be illegal, whether the material is found in videos, books, Facebook sites, tweets—you name it. Many of the more than fifty thousand persons dying each year from substance abuse are under eighteen years old. Substance abuse is child abuse.

If a person teaches a child to have sex, I consider this to be molesting a child. If you teach a child to snort opana, you are killing the child. We need a no-tampering law in place as the foundation for removing drug-abuse videos and related social-media content.

Physical (violent) child abuse is also firmly linked to substance abuse. The Child Welfare League states that children of substance abusers are three times as likely to be abused. It further notes that 40 to 80 percent of abused children have substance-abusing parents. Eight million children in the United States have substance-abusing parents. Substance abuse is child abuse. Let's pass appropriate laws to control drug-abuse-related social media, starting with the foundation of *no tampering* with pills.

A-21
Discussion of a way for the CMS not to pay pill-mill doctors

I call this the No Hybrid Practice Law for lack of a better term. Consider a doctor's perspective. You're a hardworking, dedicated doctor working long days caring for people in the office, hospitals, and rehabs/nursing homes. You meet very sick people with no insurance, so you care for them for free. At least 10 percent of your work is done for free, even in your own office. Still, you're happy to be working hard and accomplishing diligent care.

Then the CMS calls, and it audits you. They claim you billed for patients whom you didn't see, so they demand that you refund seven thousand dollars.

You know something is wrong. You not only see every patient whom you claim to, but you also don't bill sometimes. And you provide free care to patients in your office and rehabs, which you are not required to do by any law. So you request to see everything the CMS has looked at, and what do you think you find?

You find two things: On the reported days you didn't see the patients in the hospital, you actually did see them, but you put the wrong dates on progress notes. You also find some notes that are two pages long, but the patient's name is only on one page, so your government refused to pay you. Now, the last time I bought something at Walmart, I'm sure that if the date on the receipt was wrong, I didn't get the product for free. Or if a contractor doesn't put my name on the bill for a new house, I don't get the house for free, do I?

This is how a real board-certified conscientious doctor is treated by his government. I wrote a check for the money because more experienced doctors told me that I would be horribly harassed if I didn't.

Now let's look at a cash-based pain-clinic pill-mill doctor. These doctors do not have to be board certified! They bill patients for cash and never get audited. If they want tests done, they have patients bill CMS or some other payer, if possible. The patient then pays for the illegitimate medicine with Medicare or Medicaid money. If the doctor overdoses the patient, the CMS or insurance pays the hospital bill.

So when these doctors want money, they require cash with no controls or strings attached. But they still bill the government for some services. In one case, a doc billed CMS for $9 million while also getting his cash from the so-called pain patients.

If these doctors at their pill mills want to run their practices like a cash and carry store, they need to be treated like one. We should not allow illegitimate drug prescribing behavior and billing while auditing a real doctor in such a nasty manner. We have more control on many businesses than we do on cash-only pain clinics.

There is nothing wrong with making a cash-only pain clinic or any other cash-only clinic declare itself as such and require that it does not mix billing practices—that is, hybrid billing should not be allowed. Being a cash-only clinic should not allow the doctor to be held to any lower, less safe, or less fair standards than any other doctor. There would be nothing wrong with requiring a specific board certification for these doctors as well as financial standards, safety standards, documentation standards, or any number of other measures that would be expected of a doctor utilizing a large quantity of dangerous medicine. Cash versus third-party-payer status should not change safety or documentation standards. Don't you want *all* doctors in this country to be subject to the same controls so that when your child goes to a doctor you have some level of confidence in the doctor's practice? *Or* do you want a cash-only doc to be uncontrolled? You decide.

Yes, many states do now have pain-clinic laws. We need a national registry for these clinics, a set of national regulations that they must follow, and specific licensing programs. There is nothing unfair or unconstitutional about recognizing a new industry and developing regulations to keep it safe and fair.

If having the correct date on my hospital notes, or the patient name on both pages one and two of my notes is so important for my patient, then it is as important for the cash clinics also, and for the same reasons: accuracy of billing practice and patient safety.

The state of Wisconsin has taken this idea even further with its bill AB-366. This is an excellent bill that can be made national. It controls pain-clinic certification and requirements. It outlaws the use of cash for payment, which is very good because it thus requires true identification of a patient by credit card or check. The bill also requires that a medical director be named for the pain clinic—also a nice feature.

I would take this a little further and require establishment of a certificate of need (CON) to open a pain clinic. Here's why: at one point Florida was the pill-mill capital of the United States. In 2010, 650 million pills were prescribed there. Florida had 856 pain clinics. There are only sixty-seven counties in Florida. The largest county is forty-five square miles, so at most you only need four clinics in that county and perhaps about seventy-five in the whole state. A CON program would have reduced the massive large quantity of cash pill mills and the terrible problem Florida had, to less than one-tenth of its size without compromising legitimate pain patients and without spending any money on enforcement. In 2010, 1,516 people overdosed in Florida. The number grows when we factor in people who were flying and driving to Florida to get medicine and then overdosing in their home states.

This is all simple stuff to understand, and we can bring it about on a national basis. We can also allow states to opt to do it themselves—that is, take the federal laws and run systems themselves in their own states. CONs, licensing, and surveillance can be done by the state using federal guidelines or by a federal agent like the DEA or CMS.

In summary, let's make Wisconsin AB-366 national and add a CON program, a departure from hybrid billing, and some details on certification of medical directors and care providers. I would write such a law for our country.

A-22
A discussion of Megan's Law for drug pushers

At first this sounds simple: a system just like the Megan's Law for child abusers to alert parents of the whereabouts of drug pushers. But this could be abused and used as a system for drug users to find pushers, too.

To correct this possibility, we have two controls. First, the existing Megan's Law database (in my state) already has a feature whereupon any person seeking to use the system must register with name and whereabouts. We will use this also. So any attempt to abuse the system will result in disclosure of one's identity.

Second, unlike the Megan's Law database, names, photos, and addresses of pushers would not be provided to the public, just their approximate locations—perhaps the nearest intersection or the name of an apartment building or complex—to allow planning by home buyers of where to live or move to. This is all the access that political officials would need also—just enough to do budgeting for programs in their town and county.

But police and other law-enforcement officials would have access to complete information. So would school officials, in order to plan safe school activities and placement of bus stops.

Also, we would establish a cutoff level of substance found or crime charged so as not to have any persons just caught with their own drugs in the system. It's not control of addicts but control of drug pushers that we are seeking.

A-23
A discussion of the gateway-drug law

It's normal human behavior to want to do more of what makes you feel good. We want to do more of what we like and less of what we don't. We do activity that results in reward. As young children we learn to do what our parents do. We learn to live a lifestyle that we see and enjoy. The drug addict learns from other drug addicts, too. And the drug addict learns from other drug users who may not be addicts. Is that even possible, to be a drug user but not an addict? Can I use a drug properly but still influence a young person watching me to be an addict? Can a young person be influenced to become an addict even if his or her parents are not? Are there influences on young people other than their parents?

The answer to all these questions is yes, of course.

We all see the stories about the child who played golf at age three and went on to be a world-champion golfer, the child who rode a toy car and became an Indy 500 winner, or the child who rode a fire truck and later became a fire chief. Sadly, an experiment with a drug can lead a child to become an addict—and then a dead addict.

When I went to medical school in 1991, I lived in a depressed area of a big city. I chose the school because I knew that I would see more and learn more if I went to an inner-city school. Having little money, I rented a five-by-eight-foot room. Each day I would ride to school, and during the ride, I studied the city. Having lived in a rural community, it was all new to me. A smart friend of mine told me that every environment will breed a specific organism. This is true with humans as well as microorganisms: we only know what we see. As we get older, we can venture out on our own and see more. But as children, we are a captive audience. The children who live in the city only know what they see in the city, which leads me to my point about gateway drugs.

A gateway drug is one that young people try for starters. They like the experience, so they continue to use the drug, but they become dissatisfied with just that one, so they move on to drugs with more of a kick. The thing that makes the experience good for them does not have to be chemical. It could be as simple as enjoying an activity with friends or feeling that they are taking part in a better way of life. Or their feelings can be enhanced by a reduction in inhibition or anxiety, brought about by the true chemical effect of the drug. It is well established by government studies that cigarettes, alcohol, and marijuana are gateway drugs. I cannot take the anxiolytic effect out of these drugs. I cannot take the sharing of activity with their friends out of this environment. *But* I can take the feeling of "taking part in a better way of life" out of the drugs.

By this time, I hope you are asking yourself, "What is he talking about? How does smoking a cigarette or drinking an alcoholic drink have to do with a better way of life?" I'll tell you so that you will learn this and see it the way I did.

Back to medical school for the answer. I got up and drove to school in the city. Each day I saw the effects of gunshots and violence from gang fights, drug overdoses, HIV galore, hepatitis galore, alcoholism, liver failure, infections from IV-drug abuse, and I practiced medicine on their victims. Remember that's why I decided to go to an inner-city school, to see all this stuff. And since these patients don't have money or insurance, they must let medical students take care of them. I held all these things in my hands for four years and saw these people up close and personal. This is the stuff that's not in textbooks. This is the special experience of the inner-city medical school that I was looking for and am now sharing with you.

My home growing up was not like this. My town was not like this. Why? I started to explore, and I saw things in the city. They're not just city things but things that exist everywhere. It's like discovering new things about our environment.

Here is what I saw: I saw children waiting at the school-bus stop, walking on the sidewalk, or playing at a park. I saw people going to church. As I looked up, I saw signs: big signs, lots of signs, billboards, posters, advertisements—you name it.

I do photography as a hobby, and for more than twenty years, I have wanted to go back to Newark, New Jersey, and take pictures of this environment—one that breeds a specific type of organism. What the pictures would show you are the children I mentioned, loomed over by advertisements for alcohol (and tobacco at that time). In one brightly colored sign are beautiful, scantily clad women with a handsome man standing by a fantastic sports car, *drinking alcohol* as if to say, "When you buy this product, you get the car and the girls." So if I drink, I will be like that guy in the sign, right? Won't I? Won't that be my start to a picture-perfect way of life—drinking alcohol?

This is vicious false advertising that targets poor, young, impressionable people, and it promotes the use of gateway drugs. Would you want advertisements for alcohol inside your child's grade school? Of course not. Then why do we allow them to be visible at school-bus stops or school playgrounds?

These substances are firmly established as gateway drugs by our government agencies. But once again there is no full follow-through about them by these agencies. Why did we spend millions of dollars of taxpayers' money to confirm these are gateway drugs and then do nothing about exposing our children to them?

We must stop all advertising of these substances within our children's line of sight, near schools and school-bus stops, playgrounds, and other public areas where young people gather. This is the principle of my gateway law.

We would take these measures slowly over years, so as not to hurt businesses that use the existing advertising. We stopped cigarette advertising on TV and other locations, and we can eventually stop other forms of advertising for alcohol and soon possibly marijuana, too. I would suggest about a six-year or shorter plan, as follows:

1. Establish no-advertising areas around schools and bus stops, by survey.
2. Ban new signs in these areas, but allow maintenance of the old ones.
3. Allow no photographs of tobacco or alcohol products to be added to existing ones.
4. Allow no words on signs to be readable from the designated areas.
5. Ensure that the signs are gone by the end of six years.

Most towns already have laws about signs, and most collect permit money for any permanent signs. My plan would simply become blended into these laws. We would simply not allow signs advertising substances in the same way that we would not allow signs of naked people. Your town could still collect application fees and permits to place the signs appropriately, and these funds would pay for sign-surveillance programs. No increases in taxes would be needed.

We can alternatively and more simply model advertising of all gateway substances like the last round of tobacco advertising laws only a little stronger. This would be to allow only indoor point-of-sale advertising inside institutions that have a twenty-one-years-old-to-enter policy. Then you, not big industry, can control your child's exposure to these substances the way you see fit.

A-24
Discussion of the patent law

Drug dealers are now starting to manufacture more drugs here in the United States, which eliminates transportation costs into the country. If we increase activity that will limit drug imports, such as building a border wall, then manufacturing here in the United States will increase.

The drugs now being made here include fentanyl and its analogs, W-18, and there will be more. Fentanyl and W-18 are far more powerful and far deadlier than heroin or oxycodone (regardless of which cellular receptor they attach to.) Since these drugs are extremely powerful, they are diluted for sale. This means that many varying potencies are out on the street now, and continued confusion will cause more overdoses and drug deaths. I once saw a young man accidentally die in the intensive-care unit of a hospital with fentanyl while under the care of doctors and nurses. That's how dangerous this medicine is.

Regardless of what you have heard about W-18, W-15, or fentanyl, the point is that, by suppressing drug imports, we will see an increase in homemade drugs with dangerous impurities in various strengths. All sustained users of fentanyl will accidently kill themselves; it's so strong. If there is nothing left to buy but homemade fentanyl or something worse, that is what will happen. We will see one hundred thousand people die from drugs in a year, and it will be blamed on President Trump building the wall. But the truth is that we have to stop *all* drugs, not just the imported ones.

How do drug pushers know how to make drugs? It's simple; when the drug is held under patent, the US government patent office will teach them for free! Just Google fentanyl patent, and instructions on making fentanyl come up. Instructions for other patented drugs are available as well.

There is no need for this information to be so readily available and quickly accessible. It can be stored just as it traditionally was. You had to go to the patent office, sign in and provide ID, and look for it in print. True, it is still publicly available but not to individuals without ID. As things stand, even competing manufacturers in other countries can get the information instantly.

We must limit the persons who can access such information, with background checks. And have them sign contracts that clearly define both what they are permitted to do with the information and the penalties for doing anything else.

We will also need to use political bargaining with other countries to stop this flow of information on a global scale and make it a crime to disseminate the information online. In fact, we need to take patent information for *all* drugs offline because we have seen drugs that were not seen to be addictive or dangerous but were later found to be so—or at least to be associated with the drug-addiction lifestyle.

The US Patent and Trademark Office and patent services has to stop publishing how to make drugs.

A-25

A discussion of the increase of school drug-free zones to one mile and the quadruple-damages law

Many communities have school zones in which fines are higher for using guns or drugs.

In nursing homes if elderly patients are found to have suffered from malpractice or neglect, they may seek damages in court. A law is on the books that will automatically triple financial damages awarded by a jury because suffering took place in a nursing home. It was passed to place even greater responsibility than commonly expected on nursing homes to ensure that they provide good care to our beloved elderly.

I would say that our children are just as beloved, are just as vulnerable, and have more potential life in jeopardy ahead of them. So I would ask for a quadruple-damages law for any drug-related crime within a school zone. If a state doesn't agree, then the federal government can collect the remaining three-quarters of the fine and use the money for fighting drugs.

The minimum size of school zones is usually some number of feet from schools. This size should be increased to one mile, as children can easily walk or ride a bike a mile.

Why would anyone disagree with this?

A-26

A discussion of the analog law

On a sunny day in Wildwood, New Jersey, I was walking on the boardwalk. One of the stores looked interesting, so I went in. They were selling bongs in the store, and they had all kinds of stuff to smoke, too. There were things like K2 (Spice), Spice Gold, Spice Diamond, Yucatan Fire, Solar Flare, Genie, Pep Spice, and Fire 'n' Ice.

At that time they were all forms of synthetic marijuana made by humans.

The products are not real marijuana, so they are not illegal! In fact, if I invent a molecule that makes you high and can kill you, it's not illegal. Only the drugs/molecules already named in laws are illegal. So if I add a few atoms and change molecules, I am not infringing on a patent or making anything that's illegal. And I can sell my drug.

In 2011, the use of K2 was discovered by ER doctors in Dallas when three sixteen-year-old boys were brought in for having heart attacks while using it.

Where did K2 come from? It seems to have been invented by NIDA using taxpayers' money. According to a National Medical Systems report, a professor of organic chemistry was given funding to do research, and he developed it—good intentions that went bad when drug dealers learned how to make it.

One by one, each state has outlawed K2 and compounds like it, which means that many times, lawmakers unknowingly allowed a problem to start and then had to develop a law against it. Are we going to go through another K2 with W-18 or W-15 or any other time somebody invents a new recreational drug? (In January 2018 I met a patient who said she had two persons in her high school die from K2, so it's not going away.)

Within this system, we will have problem after problem with every new invented molecule. To counteract the trend, states have developed analog laws, which seek to outlaw any molecules that are close to existing drugs of abuse or are analogous to them. The federal government does have Public Law 99-570, the Controlled Substance Analogue Enforcement Act of 1986. This law was tested in *USA v. Damon S. Forbes*; it failed to protect the public and was deemed void by vagueness. Remember the term "void by vagueness," and ask yourself why I want to apply engineering to countering the drug epidemic.

The law was also used in *USA v. Washam*, and it worked because "there was only one difference between the two molecules on one side." This is ridiculous, and I will explain why by example.

If we add a single life-giving atom of oxygen to a life-giving water molecule, we get hydrogen peroxide, a liquid that kills everything it touches. So here are two clearly analogous molecules in the eyes of a jury with no chemistry education, but one you need to live and the other will kill you. Nitroglycerin saves the lives of heart-attack patients, but if you dilute the nitroglycerin in dirt, you get a dynamite explosive—the same molecule packaged in a different way. Are these analogs? Of course not. The concept of the analog law is useless. It must have been developed by someone who was told to go write an analog law, who did the best possible with the knowledge he or she had.

What we do need is a well-written law designed to stop production of dangerous, psychoactive drugs by street-drug dealers. Molecular structure means nothing here; let the drug be defined by its effect on persons and animals. Any person producing a dangerous, psychoactive drug and distributing it to people or animals will be in violation of the law. We would retain the term "animal" to stop people from buying drugs "for their dogs." The definition of "dangerous, psychoactive" will be simple. It should not be defined by a long FDA study because drug dealers produce new substances too fast. It will be defined as follows:

> If an individual is required to seek medical attention or displays dangerous behavior that results in the summoning of authorities, such as law enforcement, or the injuring of himself or herself or others by using the new substance, then the substance is to be considered illegal and its producer to be a manufacturer of illegal drugs.

People like me should write laws for lawyers to use instead of having lawyers write laws that don't address real problems. Scrap the analog law; I will write the law we do need.

A-28
Discussion of the implementation of a monthly patient-condition monitoring system

I have privileges to write prescriptions for a medicine called Clozaril. In order for me to do so, I have to read the regulations regarding this medicine (FDA POS*7*222) and agree to test patient labs every month. Even then I must fax a copy of the labs to the drug manufacturer each month. If the labs are normal, then the manufacturer will send a one-month supply of the medicine.

This procedure ensures that the doctor knows the side effects of the medicine, tests for them, and discovers whether the patient is suffering from side effects. Only then, and only on a month-by-month basis, can the patient receive the medicine.

Monitoring the use of benzodiazepine and narcotic medicines is more complex but not at all impossible. By simply making the patient go to the doctor each month, the doctor can assess the patient's general health and check for side effects of the medicine. Laboratory tests would be useful for these patients as well as special tests for those suffering from specific disorders, such as sleep apnea patients on pain meds.

For example, a patient takes narcotics three times a day and benzodiazepine two times a day. Blood tests are done to check levels of the medicines. A zero blood level for either one of these medicines indicates that the patient is not taking it, which should prompt a discussion between doctor and patient. The doctor needs to ask about daytime sleepiness, constipation, cognitive function and employment, and physical activity and driving while on the medicine, whether the medicine is stored safely in the house, and whether children are present.

Simply put, these medicines are clearly the most dangerous ones we prescribe, which warrants a monthly check on the patient's health while on them—just like for Clozaril. Some 950 deaths have been attributed to Clozaril in the last twenty-seven years or so, and we even have an in-place system to control it and the doctors who prescribe it. Meanwhile, we have more than one thousand times as many deaths from narcotics and benzos and no system to control them. You decide: should we have such a system?

If we did have such a system, it would include a standardized set of exam criteria, labs and questions designed to find the patients who are having trouble with the medicines or would be safer with lower doses or other medicines. Then it would ensure doctor- and patient-implemented changes and good follow-up.

This is so simple: do you want a doctor to give narcotics and benzos to your sons or daughters without checking them before each refill?

A-29
Discussion of the implementation of a pay for performance system

CMS has many pay-for-performance systems, which are designed to lower the reimbursement paid to doctors and hospitals if they do not do a good job. For example, the CMS evaluates hospital care for seven different illnesses; if it finds that a given hospital must readmit patients back to the hospital within thirty days for the same illness, the hospital is paid less. This gives the hospital an incentive to get you well and keep you well. Hospitals have initiated systems to stay in touch with patients and follow their progress after discharge. Patients who were treated for, say, heart failure, will be introduced to a heart-failure team, the members of which will seek to improve the patients' chances of staying healthy.

When a person is admitted to a hospital with a substance-abuse-related issue, things are very different. These persons are usually viewed as unwanted problem patients. Minimal effort is made to help them, and a maximum effort is made to discharge them, usually with no follow-up planned. Often there are few, if any, funded community programs to help these persons. Some are given a taxi ride back to a street corner where they were found or to a shelter.

In the meantime, the CMS is following readmission as a measure of performance. In one small study of eighteen illnesses, in one state "drug and alcohol abuse" had the highest readmission rate, even higher than diabetes, a disease that is treatable but not curable. If you wanted to follow a hospital's readmission rate for an illness, wouldn't you want to start with the illness that has the highest readmission rate? These readmission rates vary by gender, location, time span studied and other factors. One study of readmissions for substance abuse states, "Diagnosis and hospital readmission rates of female veterans with substance abuse related disorders" (*Psychiatric Services* 1995; (46)9) found a 44 percent readmission rate over one year. The overall thirty-day readmission rate for substance abuse seems to be about 15 percent (admittedly not the highest of all diseases). Then there is the death rate too.

Data from Maryland showed that 59 percent of all drug-overdose deaths occurred in patients who were admitted to the ER in the past year for overdose. Some were admitted more than ten times. That means that almost six out of ten persons who died of drug overdose identified themselves to the health-care system. No other illness so clearly identifies its victims while they are still otherwise healthy. This data calls out for action to identify susceptible persons and take action to help them the same way we identify and control readmissions for other illnesses.

Although helping these persons is difficult, the ability to identify them is extremely easy and calls out for a pay-for-performance measure, a measure of some activity to help prevent further substance abuse, even if that activity is just a mandatory referral into a funded social network or other social assistance and education program. We would also provide them with a mandated package of educational materials, such as those described in item 11. Line item 38 has related detail regarding discharge of substance abusers from the hospital.

The pay-for-performance system would be modeled just like existing systems for other illnesses. (Whether drug abuse is an actual illness or not is beside the point.) If a patient is readmitted for substance abuse within a given time frame, then the hospital reimbursement will go down. If the patient dies of substance abuse within a given time frame, then the reimbursement goes down more.

The point is that users who are coming to the hospital are usually costing taxpayers money every time they visit the ER. Their condition has the highest readmit rate and the highest death-after-discharge rate, and they are the most easily identifiable persons who will die from this problem within a year. Yet the government puts zero effort into controlling how hospitals deal with them.

A-30
Discussion of a revised national prescription defense law

There is a very subtle but disgusting activity taking place in our country. As you read this, keep in mind an image of a crooked doctor running a pill mill or an unwitting doctor who gives a patient a legitimate one-month-supply prescription for a narcotic pain medicine once a year. Then think of a person who deals narcotics on the street and a lawyer who unwittingly or wittingly defends this person when he or she is arrested for that activity. What we have is a doctor-dealer-lawyer connection. States do have pill-carrying laws to try to break this connection, but the laws are poorly written and inadequate.

Persons get away with selling narcotics on the street every day. This is an example how: Once a year you go to a doctor and complain of a fall that resulted in bad pain. You get checked out and discharged. Keep in mind that nearly every person has an abnormal back x-ray or MRI. (I have been looking at such films for twenty-five years, so I know.) There is always a finding that could cause pain; medical literature has proved this. But you can't see pain on an x-ray. So, to help with pain, the doctor gives you Motrin, cyclobenzaprine, and oxycodone.

You start selling oxycodone on the street. And ten months later, you get caught with the pills and arrested or fined.

You hire a lawyer, who gets the charges thrown out. How? The lawyer tells the judge that you have a legitimate script for oxycodone and that the pills were your own. You cannot be arrested for carrying your own pills.

Do you see the abnormal logic here? The doctor gave you, say, thirty pills to be used because of that one injury. Now you tell the judge that your back hurts so much that you must carry the pills with you. You use them so much that you can't leave the house without them, *yet* those thirty pills have lasted for ten *months*. This is the prescription defense, and some lawyers love getting paid to protect drug dealers with it. They run ads recruiting dealers to defend. It's simple math: thirty pills will only last thirty days. They tell the judge that your back got better in a week. Then, just the day before you got arrested, you hurt it again, so you started taking the old pills again.

You can also get refills every month and sell them so that you always have a current script. But that still doesn't explain the need to carry the pills around with you. Some pills should never be used outside your home. See the Carry Law section, earlier in this volume.

The prescription defense represents an immoral manipulation of poorly written laws. I will show you how to stop this backdoor defense of drug dealers. There are many ways to write an effective law. I would propose a six-tier law with the six levels of expiration dates for the prescription. The most stringent level would be as described in the Carry Law section for long-acting narcotics and other dangerous, long-acting meds. It would not allow these pills outside the house ever. The lowest level would allow the prescription to be used for six months. The DEA would set the levels for the pills. A doctor or state or county could individually raise a level of control (by shortening the expiration time) but not lower it.

Such a process would allow the DEA to set a cap on or expiration date for the prescription defense, allow a doctor to lower the cap (shorten the time to expiration of a given prescription) for specific causes of pain, and allow the states and even counties to raise the level of control (again shorten the expiration time,), if needed, to combat a local problem. But it would still allow a needy patient to get enough pain medicine for use at home and away from home.

Here's how it would work: When a doctor gives you a prescription for a narcotic pain medicine or any other dangerous drug with abuse potential, the doctor will click on an expiration date for use outside the house on the screen in his electronic medical record (EMR). One of the following boxes would be checked:

1) *No* use outside the house
2) Use for one week outside the house
3) Use for one month outside the house
4) Use for sixty days outside the house
5) Use for six months outside the house

This would be in place in addition to the overall expiration date for the prescription. See requirements in the Carry Law section. And remember that we have EMR now, so all this can be done by clicking on a screen and saved for following scripts also, so the doctor does not have to do all the clicking over again the next time he or she sees this patient. All pertinent data and dates would be printed on the pill bottle when you get it.

As such, no drug dealer would be able to use an old prescription as an excuse (defense in court) to carry an unlimited number of pills around to sell. Another engineering roadblock to drug abuse would succeed without the use or expense of public lawyers and courts. The police would simply look at the bottle and access the national database to confirm the data on the bottle. Counterfeiting a script or bottle label would be impossible, because it wouldn't show up in the national database. Counterfeiting would be undone by another engineering roadblock.

The prescription-defense loophole for drug dealers would disappear, but patients' rights to obtain and carry pills in accordance with their doctors' prescriptions are preserved.

While we are on this subject, it's very important to understand who drug dealers are. We tend to think of shady guys standing in an alley selling cocaine. This is often true. But please keep in mind that a person who obtains something like sixty narcotic pills every month for pain and starts selling to friends the pills that he or she doesn't need, is a drug dealer. And that friend is just as likely to create a drug addict or kill one as the shady character in the alley. Remember, 87 percent of drug addicts started out using prescription medicine for themselves or from someone with a prescription.

A-31
Discussion of a ceiling on the number of prescriptions that any one doctor, nurse practitioner, or advanced-practice nurse may write in a day

Doctors are busy, hardworking people. At times, I would work twenty-seven days in a row without a day off. Then I would take one day off and repeat the cycle. I would do up to 650 patient visits per month.

Let's do some math. Remember that the problem to solve is, how many prescriptions does a real doctor write in a day, month, or year?

Working six days a week (6) for twelve hours a day ($\times$ 12) for fifty weeks a year ($\times$ 50) is thirty-six hundred hours of work. So if I see a patient every fifteen minutes (3,600 $\times$ 4), that's 14,400 patients. If I write a long-acting and a short-acting narcotic for each patient, assuming every patient is a new or refill patient (2 $\times$ 14,400), that's 28,800 narcotic prescriptions in one year. Clearly this is an extreme example; no real doctor does this many narcotics prescriptions, but keep reading, and you will see my point.

Now, the USDOJ Northern District of Alabama recently published a report about a doctor ("Huntsville Pill Mill Doctor Sentenced to 15 Years in Prison for Illegal Prescribing and Health Care Fraud," February 7, 2017) who prescribed narcotics 110,013 times in one year. The scenario that I presented about working thirty-six hundred hours and writing two narcotic scripts for every patient I meet and only giving each patient fifteen minutes for the visit and paperwork is completely ridiculous in that it is extreme—and it only resulted in 28,800 scripts. Why would we ever allow a doctor to write more than that, about ninety-six narcotics pre-scriptions per day? This doctor wrote 423 narcotic prescriptions every day for a year. Are we to believe that he saw 210 patients per day for a year? Year after year? And why did it take five years to catch him? We are spending hundreds of millions of taxpayer dollars to stop these pill-mill doctors, and these are the results we get. If a company took five years to find an employee stealing 423 items a day, it would fire the CEO. The USDOJ actually thought they did a good job on this case. Does this sound like a good system to you? Does this sound like a good job by the USDOJ to you? And this is only one example.

How can we ensure that this type of pill-mill doctor will *never* practice medicine again?

Doing so would be very easy!

It can be accomplished without spending one dime of taxpayer money! Just follow my plan.

Items 1 and 2 refer to a national database for prescription monitoring. It's a computer—that is, a machine—so you can't fool it. We would simply put a ceiling on the number of narcotic scripts that a doctor can write in a day, and bye-bye pill mills. It's that simple. No real doctor would ever argue with a limit like eighty or even fewer narcotic prescriptions per day. Not even a real pain-clinic doctor would argue with that figure. It's really no more complex than that: just follow this plan, specifically items 1, 2, 21, and 31, and the pill mills will go away, at no cost to taxpayers.

Note: The limit must be set at daily or twelve hours to prevent multiple doctors rotating into a clinic from writing seven hundred scripts in one or two days at any given location. We will also need a weekly limit of five days. This regulation would be simple and easy to do. There are many ways to assess the number of scripts a given type of doctor should be able to write in a day. We can also set up a hotline for a doctor to call if he or she hits a limit and still has a legitimate case to write a script for.

A-32

Discussion on maximized research and development of nonnarcotic pain-control medicine and nonbenzo anxiety medicine

No one wants to invest time and money in something that doesn't give a return. Pharmaceutical companies are no different. They want to invent medicine that can be sold for a profit. And once they have done so, they are less likely to invest in research to develop a medicine to replace it. Why would a pharmaceutical company do research to invent a medicine that will compete with the sales of one of its own medicines? Nor will a pharmaceutical company do research on a medicine that will not be paid for by insurance companies. So we can expect that little or no research will be done on any safer alternatives to narcotics if (1) we are already buying lots of narcotics and (2) the companies know that alternatives are not likely to be paid for by CMS or insurance companies. This is the situation that we are in today.

It would make sense to do more research and development on nonnarcotic pain medicine. The companies would need to know that the new medicines will be paid for by Medicaid Medicare and private payers. It would also be appropriate for any company selling narcotics to be encouraged to research new, safer, nonpsychoactive pain medicine and treatments. It would further make sense to require these companies to do the research.

Now I suspect I have your attention. You may be thinking that we can't make a company do research on new drugs or require any such spending on new medicine. But we can, and we do all the time, every day. Our country decided to fight air pollution, and we required functional design characteristics of the cars we drive to not pollute. Further, we made these requirements *before* the companies had the technology to meet them. And we gave them a deadline on when to invent the technology. We also required that they continue to provide cars with high gas mileage, even though not all car buyers might want those cars. And if a car company lied, we fined it. Cases in point: General Motors was fined $45 million for a pollution issue, Honda was fined $12.6 million in fees and required to pay $4.5 million in pollution-reducing projects, and Ford was required to pay $7.8 million, recall cars at a cost to the company of $1.3 million, spend $1.5 million in pollution-reduction projects, and purchase nitrogen-oxide credits for $2.5 million. Thus the auto industry works and pays for protecting the environment from its own pollution. And there are any number of other industries that pay fees and meet government requirements to stay safe and clean.

How's this for a crazy comparison? Most cities and states now have a "percent for art law" that requires a builder to spend 1 percent of construction costs on art outside the new building. So if a narcotics manufacturer decides to build a new building where this law is in force, it must spend money on art but not necessarily on research for safer medicine. Is that your priority—art over patient safety?

Let's reevaluate the pharmaceutical industry regarding these priorities. It is an industry that in the past has always risen to help humanity. The problems we have with addiction to prescription drugs like oxycodone and anxiety drugs is a new problem that has taken many years to come to the forefront. But now it is there, so we need to start to manage the industry just as we do the automotive industry. We know that automobiles are wonderful things, but they do harm our environment. So we put controls on the industry that increase the complexity and cost of the cars, but we are willing to sustain these for the sake of a better environment. Let's do the same thing with the pharmaceutical industry—give pharmaceutical companies a set of regulations and goals to meet. Their goals would be to develop and distribute more nonnarcotic pain meds and nonbenzo anxiety meds, to protect our young people. It makes perfect sense.

I could write a set of such regulations and build in a slow, steady increase in safety over the years to come. If the auto industry can do it, so can the pharmaceutical industry.

Here's how it could work. First, we set up pain-control standards for multiple common medical problems like low back pain, arthritis pain, diabetic neuropathy pain, fibromyalgia, and others. Next, we set up a ladder of measures of efficacy such as MME (milligrams of morphine equivalent) of morphine-equivalent analgesic, and functional parameters such as the ability to walk pain-free, the ability to return to work, and others. We also set up measures of respiratory depression and wakefulness, using, for example, the maintenance of wakefulness test. This is a test that can be done in an outpatient setting to see if a medicine causes drowsiness or sleep. More information on this test can be found on the American Association of Sleep Medicine website.

Then we set up a time line spanning years, with goals to meet with new medicine. The goals will reflect increasing efficacy measures while maintaining good wakefulness and no respiratory depression.

Last—and this is important—companies will be assured that any medicine or procedure developed to meet these safer goals will be paid for by insurers and CMS. And as new, safer pain and anxiety medicine is developed, the older and more dangerous medicines will be removed from the market. I would start with one goal to be to replace five-milligram oxycodone with a nonrespiratory-suppressant medicine in five years. The company that invents this new medicine will have great incentive, as millions of units will be sold the first day it is on the market. And Percocet will be removed from the market.

Thus we incentivize safety instead of ignoring it, just as we did with the auto industry.

A-33
Discussion of the required use of, and third-party payment of, nonnarcotic pain medicine and modalities both in hospitals and other outpatient services

When there is a drought, local government usually enacts a temporary law to stop people from wasting water, perhaps banning the watering of lawns, the washing of cars, or water brooming. When there is a snow emergency, we see rules about not parking on snow-emergency roads. When there is an epidemic, we have seen travel bans and even quarantines of people. With the Ebola epidemic, we saw the president of the United States order both. The Ebola epidemic of 2014 killed 11,315 people over twenty-one months, or 6,465 per year. Only eleven cases were in the United States, and seven of them came here with the disease. Only two Americans died, but the president of our country got involved and wrote laws instituting travel bans and using taxpayers' money to develop a vaccine. The Nebraska Medical Center spent $1.16 million on two patients. Senator Schumer requested $20 million to pay for New York's bill of $14.6 million to care for one patient (no, that's not a typo—one patient), to monitor others, and to prepare hospitals for Ebola. The president's emergency funding for Ebola was $6.2 billion. Eleven cases with two deaths generated $6.2 billion tax spent.

Now back to earth. In recent years, we have seen five hundred thousand people die of drug abuse in the United States. Now we are at more than sixty thousand deaths per year, not to mention cases of drug-related illness or hospitalization. What is the government doing about this? If eleven cases of Ebola brought about spending more than $6 billion, then why do we not require doctors, hospitals, and insurance companies to spend anything to prevent the sixty thousand deaths? GlaxoSmithKline spent $325 million on a vaccine company and had the company make an Ebola vaccine. Johnson and Johnson spent $200 million on their effort. Profectus BioSciences got a $17 million grant to work on a vaccine. (You can read more about the great efforts made by companies and governments around the world to develop vaccines for Ebola in articles like the one in the *Economist*, "Give It a Shot," October 30, 2014. And many others.)

The epidemic of drug deaths we are witnessing is like a reverse drought—that is, there is a large use of narcotic and benzodiazepine and associated danger with them. So we would expect our government to request less use of these meds and facilitate the use of safer, alternative medicine. With our third-party-payer system, payers (i.e., CMS and insurance companies) and providers (i.e., doctors and hospitals) would have to be paid for and use, respectively, every possible alternative medicine to reduce the use of narcotics and benzos. And one would expect a similarly large research effort like the Ebola research to take place to find new, safer medicines.

Study the numbers you have just read. Compare the number of cases to the money spent, and note the people involved in the lawmaking process. Now compare those cases to the current epidemic of more than sixty thousand lives lost in the United States every year.

We do have alternative medicine now, and I see much possibility for further research, but I don't see any "Ebola-like" response.

With regard to alternative medicine, an example is that doctors have asked many hospital systems to use intravenous Tylenol as a pain medicine instead of narcotics. But the hospital systems will often not pay for it. We have hospital-system CEOs earning salaries like $12 million a year and not willing to spend money on intravenous Tylenol because it costs $35 a dose. Even when it cost $14, they wouldn't pay for it. Keep in mind that the cost of delivering a one-milligram dose of Dilaudid, including starting the IV line, is about $144, with $7 for the drug. It would increase to $172 for Tylenol.

When it's not raining enough, you are not allowed to water your lawn. But when fifty people are dying every nine hours, a hospital CEO who earns millions of dollars a year can continue to refuse to conserve narcotics because it will cost the hospital twenty-eight dollars a dose. Your government does not fund research for alternative medicine. And insurance companies can decide to pay for only what they want to.

Based on data from an AcelRx study, I calculate a cost of $167,071 dollars per hospital to replace every IV dose of narcotic in their ER with Tylenol. If we split this cost between the CEO and the owners of the hospital, do you think they would miss it? Would it have that great an effect on a CEO's $2 million bonus? The hospital used in the above example has a CEO earning a total pay of more than $5 million, including $2 million in bonuses. When the cost of a dose of Tylenol went from $14 to $35, he stopped using it.

Did you notice that the Ebola epidemic only lasted twenty-one months? Our opioid epidemic has been going on for years and is still increasing. In the United States alone we have lost more than five hundred thousand lives; the present rate of lives lost in this country is more than ten times as fast as the lives lost to Ebola in all six affected countries combined.

Again, to review: there was one case of Ebola in New York, and the state spent $14 million on hospital systems and preparedness. But when perhaps one thousand lives are lost every year in one state, a hospital CEO is not required to spend thirty-five dollars a dose for an alternate medication, to conserve narcotics.

You decide: Should the insurance companies and hospitals be required to pay for nonnarcotic pain medicine to save sixty thousand lives per year? Or should we save that money to spend six billion dollars on a vaccine to save two Americans, while letting hospital CEOs keep their million-dollar paychecks and give your son or daughter cheap narcotics?

Or look at it this way: if you were a hospital CEO earning $6 million per year, could you easily cut your pay to $5.85 million to help stem the opioid epidemic?

A-36
Discussion of antidoctor-shopping laws

You now know that some persons shop doctor to doctor within a state and from state to state. States do have a computer system to monitor prescriptions, and some states are connected by computer network, *but* I, someone who uses my state's system every day, see *no* enforcement against untoward activities by doctors or patients. And when I find a patient who has seen several doctors for narcotics, there is no way to tell whether the patient merely forgot to inform me or is a drug dealer looking for another doctor to supply drugs. Let's talk realistically now. Do you actually think a doctor is going to call the police on a patient? Ask any police officer if he or she would arrest a person who went to two doctors in the same week. I think that lawmakers know that laws against doctor shopping are completely unenforceable, but write them in a good effort.

Yet every state has anti–doctor-shopping laws, and nationally we are told to apply antifraud laws and mandatory-disclosure laws. These are laws that essentially say that people cannot lie to their doctors—or to anyone else, for that matter—for personal gain. Can you imagine what it would cost to call the police every time a doctor caught a person going to two doctors to get narcotics or benzo medicine, factoring in police, court, jail, and personal costs? And would it do any good to put a people hooked on Percocet in jail, where they can meet a heroin dealer? This concept of anti–doctor-shopping laws is frankly ridiculous, unused, and unusable junk produced by lawmakers who tried to do something constructive. It's like leaving the safe at a bank unlocked and putting up a sign that says, "Keep out." Patients also go to different pharmacies with different scripts in different states to evade the system. Get it? You cannot police millions of people in doctors' offices.

So how can we stop the doctor shopping? You and I are affected by computer systems that monitor us every day in many ways. If you use E-ZPass and you don't pay your bill, the computer invalidates your pass. Simple; no police or court is needed. When you use your credit card, the same thing happens; when you reach your limit, the card stops working. If you don't pay your cell-phone bill, your phone stops working. If you don't pay your PayPal bill, PayPal rejects any further purchases. These are all simple, computer-driven consequences. And you accept them all without major complaint. So why do we as a nation protect our money with engineered roadblocks controlled by a computer but let people obtain enough drugs to kill our children at the next party they go to? I'll tell you why: it's because these roadblocks protect companies' money, not ours. No company or agency will develop a system to protect you or your child unless it is forced to or if doing so saves it money. This principle is also embodied in previous items 3, 21, 38.

Specifically, do you see how a national computer system with limits on monthly dosages and the number of scripts the doctor may write is the same as your credit-card company's policy? It is an engineering answer to much drug abuse, especially of the prescription drugs that get 87 percent of addicts hooked on drugs. The doctor enters your script in his EMR system, and the computer allows the correct amount of medicine to be distributed and no more. Simple.

The computer would also find the patients who are still going to multiple doctors and trying to get more narcotics. And it will find the doctors who constantly try to write too many scripts. Again, some of this is in place now, but it needs to be national, centralized, and to include Canada if it is going to work.

In summary, anti–doctor-shopping laws will *never* work; forget them. Let's use a computer as a tool to control drugs like we control corporate money. The computer system will collect the patient's activity, so when a person gets narcotics from one doctor and the next day sees another, the computer will not allow a second prescription to be filled. In addition, all doctors involved will be notified that this patient is seeing multiple doctors before his or her medicine has run out. That way, doctors will be able to identify this person as someone who needs help with a substance-abuse problem and/or some other form of medical help.

Can we make this control even better? Yes, let's factor in item 37, the lock-in laws.

A-38
A discussion of overdose discharge planning

Just about every emergency room in the country sees drug-overdose patients every day. Some are treated and admitted to the hospital; some are treated and sent home or discharged. Some are discharged and unfortunately go home and die that day. Why would a good doctor discharge a patient only to have him or her die that day or soon after? There are several reasons. I have authored a hospital policy/protocol for the treatment of alcoholic patients and know that doing the same thing for drug-overdose patients is harder and more complex. What follows is my plan for a national program to collect information and a complete detailed policy and protocol for how to treat drug-overdose patients in the ER so that when they are discharged, they don't go home and die that day. I have authored this by first collecting information on deaths from government studies, case reports, and my personal experience.

When we discharge an overdose patient, we need to think of three aspects of what will happen next:

- The chemistry of the drugs involved, such as their effect on the body, how long they will last, and their delayed effects. Will this person stop breathing again in a few hours? Will there be later effects on the brain or other organs?
- The possibility of another overdose, just like how we anticipate another reaction in allergy patients. It needs to be planned for; patients and their caregivers should receive training.
- Social aspects, such as whether the patient can get help with rehab or even call 911 later, if need be.

INTRODUCTION

This is one of the most difficult subjects in my plan. It is complicated because there are so many variables. Some of the concepts in this plan are of great interest to hospital doctors, others are more for families and drug addicts. Not everything in this section will be pleasant to read. And you will not agree with it all. Try to understand that I am trying to design a program that will not lose a single life to drug overdose and that such a program will have to place responsibility on all parties, from doctors to family and addicts. You must understand that doctors and hospitals can do tremendous work to help a drug addict. But without family support, this work will not help, and a life may still be lost. Saving a life from drug addiction is *not* all about test labs, chemicals, and cell receptors. It is about helping each other. If you think I can teach a hospital to save your child, you are wrong. If you know that I can help teach a hospital *and* you to work together as a team to save your loved one, then continue reading.

I have lost patients, and I will always think that I could have done something different to not lose them. In this section I am putting together bits and pieces of research, data, and experience to create a plan on how to discharge overdose patients from the hospital and not have them die hours later. First, we need to clearly define the problem, as I have said so many times. Then we must look for strong engineering answers to the problems. With this particular problem, the answers get intensely personal and emotional. We are now at the point of the rubber meeting the road. In most of my plan I speak about pill control, medicine, doctors, drug resellers, and patients. Now we have the heart of the problem in our hands, the very troubled persons whom we are trying to save. They are sick, on the brink of death, and friends and family may not be there. They can't think straight because they are on drugs, and we are trying to save them. Think about it. It's very clear the ER can't save them. All it can do is make them breathe again. When unconscious drug addicts wake up in the ER, do you know what they are? Drug addicts, still. Sounds cruel, doesn't it? I told you, you will not like everything I have to say. But until you understand that one concept, you will not be prepared to join the ER team to save your loved one. Stop reading, and think about what your loved one was on the day of overdose and what he or she was when resuscitated in the ER. When you are strong enough to admit that he or she is still a drug addict, then you will not only be ready to be a team member with the ER but you will also be the team leader. And I will be proud to give you and the hospital a game plan to win.

This is the most technical and complex item in my plan.

Evaluating the Problem with Discharges

I developed a protocol for the care of alcohol-withdrawal patients in the hospital that was similar to this care protocol for overdose patients. After researching hundreds of journal articles/studies, I found twenty-six studies that were very useful. The end protocol on how to care for an alcohol-withdrawal patient worked extremely well. However, the problem of how to care for an overdose patient is more complex. Alcoholics use only one drug, alcohol. The overdose patient uses unknown drugs, multiple drugs, and various routes of administration. The drugs are of unknown purity on the street, and even when the user uses a pharmaceutical drug like OxyContin, if he snorts it, it is first crushed or ground into variously sized particles. The particles are breathed in and deposit into various parts of the respiratory tract. The smallest particles that go deep into the lungs are absorbed into the blood fast. But the larger particles that stick in the trachea will dissolve later. Also, when the user takes oral pills, pharmacokinetics, that is, how the medicine enters and leaves the bloodstream, is changed by the fact that the user took so much. So data that medical personnel learn about how long these medicines last is of no use, because the data are based on taking the proper dose. At normal doses of opioid, the drugs are often cleared by first-order kinetics, meaning that a given amount of the drug will leave the body each hour. But in some overdose patients the clearance goes to zero order for some time, meaning that, for a given time, the drug will simply stay in the body; its level will not change at first.

Here is a real-life example from one of my patients who snorted cocaine. He was admitted for supraventricular tachycardia (SVT) and put in the hospital PCU on a heart monitor. His EKG was abnormal, and we kept him in the hospital. As we were getting ready to let him go forty-eight hours after admission, he went back into symptomatic SVT. I felt that this was from cocaine particles still in his lungs, so I treated him with two milligrams of Ativan IV. Now, if you're a cardiologist, you know that this medicine will not correct an SVT. But Ativan is a near-perfect antidote for cocaine, so I gave the med. It worked like magic. Its success proved that there was still an effect from the cocaine forty-eight hours later.

If you want to see published data in support of this decision, see the *NEJM* (*New England Journal of Medicine*) article about narcotic overdoses that last 120 hours. (*NEJM* 2012;367 146–155)

Let's look at "the pitfalls to treating" and releasing overdose patients, again, according to studies published in the above *NEJM* article (1 through

5 below. Others are from many other publications and from my practical experience).

1. Some medical personnel seem to have a false understanding that naloxone, an overdose-reversal medication, truncates opioid respiratory depression. It only blocks it for a short time.
2. Some believe that the dose of naloxone needed to restore respiration correlates with the dose of the narcotic taken. It does not.
3. Medical personnel associate peak plasma concentration levels, again, with the dose of drug taken, but remember where those particles or pills are. Plasma concentration means nothing. Blood level may be low because the drug is still in the bowels or the lungs.
4. Early acetaminophen toxicity often goes unrecognized when we are all concentrating on narcotics. Recall that many pills contain acetaminophen.

    Here are some added pitfalls that I have found on research, were shared with me, or I have seen.
5. Medical personnel get used to working with older, sicker patients and can mistake a physical or lab parameter as normal when it is not normal for a healthy young person. This may be one of the more important mistakes we make.
6. Some medical personnel think addicts tell the truth about what they took and when they took it. Wrong.
7. Drug addicts think they know what they took and how much of it. Wrong again.
8. Delayed bad effects of a drug overdose can occur up to forty days (not hours) later; see articles on delayed posthypoxic leukoencephalopathy and flexion myopathy. (*Journal of Clinical Neuroscience* 2012; 19(7): 1060–1062)
9. Parents and guardians may not be aware of a need for training. Even the best parent or guardian cannot physically access a patient after leaving the hospital, not without training. (We will get them training.)

10. Friends of drug addicts likely don't know how to do CPR. (We'll need to train them.)
11. Telling the addict, "Stop doing drugs" is not a discharge plan.
12. Opioid overdose is easy to treat: just keep them breathing until they go home. Wrong. One study found that even among the overdose patients admitted to the ICU, there was a 10 percent mortality rate (based on 2015 data on more than four million ICU admits.)
13. If an overdose patient refuses admission, he or she will be fine. Because the patient is awake now. Wrong again: One in a thousand who walks away from EMTs in the field refusing treatment will die, even in the field after receiving naloxone from EMTs. Patients who are brought to the ER are sicker than those who awaken and refuse transport to the ER. Don't apply field data to ER patients.
14. The injection-drug user is more like to die after discharge because this is a dangerous way to take drugs. Wrong yet again: oral agents last the longest and require the longest observation in the hospital.
15. There is nothing you can do; they will just go do drugs again. Clearly wrong again.
16. When addicts' eyes are closed, they are sleeping in the ER. Wrong again. They are more likely still under the influence of the drug. All the existing safe-for-discharge data require subjects to be "awake and alert in the absence of verbal or tactile stimuli." The key word is "absence." So if you wake up an overdose patient to ask if he or she wants to go home you are not following anyone's or any medical publication's advice or protocol. This is hard to understand and difficult to apply in real life, so read it several times.
17. You can't get sued for malpractice if addicts go home and die. Not true.
18. There are lots of seemingly good studies showing that it's safe to give naloxone and discharge the overdose patient. Also not true: please remember that a real medical study is large and complex— that is, with large numbers of patients versus controls. Controlled

follow-up of known medicines involved careful data recording review boards, etc. There are none now and likely never will be such studies. There are only articles and not studies in the real sense of the meaning.

19. Toxicology tests will tell us what the overdose patient took to overdose on. Simply wrong: these are the least important tests. For example, we now have pharmacologic fentanyl and four analogs of it on the street, and none has been tested. Nor have W-15 or K2 or many others. There will always be new substances of abuse that we don't have tests for. The USDOJ has listed more than fifty drugs of abuse, and I can add a dozen more. Only the oldest few are tested for in any hospital.

One author I read said, "Treat the patient not the poison" (Steve Weinman, RN, BSN, CEN). In other words, patient care and decision to discharge are not to be based on a tox-screen test. They should be based on correct evaluation of the whole patient.

ERs discharge patients every day, so why do I want to review and control overdose discharges? Here's why: a very large study (*British Medical Journal*, 2017; Feb 1; 356:j239) shows that if we look at all discharges and look for death soon after discharge, we find 0.12 percent of patients die within seven days of discharge. Another 2.3 percent died from narcotic overdose of pain meds given for muscle and/or bone pain—that is, they were not drug addicts but just normal persons who got pain meds from the hospital. Of the overdose patients, 8.4 percent died in the first two days, and 85 percent of these deaths were due to cardiac problems.

So we are pushing eighty times more likely to die after discharge for overdose than for any illness. Considering that the overdose patient is much younger than the average patient, this is a very bad record and an indication that we are doing something wrong. Hospitals with the lowest admission rates had the highest death rates indicating that we need to admit more.

When we compare different hospitals to each other, what do we find? We find that a small increase in admission rate resulted in a great reduction in death after discharge. In other words, good hospitals correctly identify the most at-risk patients. It was necessary to admit only a few to save them—around 8.4 percent of them. Next, we find that hospitals that charged a little more money also had a greater reduction in death. Perhaps they did a few more tests—x-rays, EKG, and so on—to identify those most at risk of death. In other words, we find there are ways to improve many, and it doesn't cost much.

Our present state of the art of discharge of the overdose patient is that the patient is more likely to die after discharge from the ER for overdose than after having major high-risk surgery. Let's improve this.

Let's divide this problem up into time segments, looking at (1) what happens to an overdose victim who has just arrived at the ER, (2) what happens while the victim is there, (3) what happens when the victim is discharged, and (4) what happens after the victim leaves.

1. On arrival at the ER

   All data from the family and paramedics must be entered and saved, especially measurement from the Glasgow coma scale (GCS) at the scene, meds given and times given, length of time the patient is estimated to have been intoxicated, and detailed vitals.

   Collect data from any source of meds available that the patient may have in possession or be on. Collect medical history and names of all known doctors of the patient, including especially a family doctor. Bring all available prescription bottles into the ER.

   Tests to administer: CBC CHEM-7 creatinine kinase troponin-1, EKG and CXR vitals, GCS level, pulse oximeter, capnography reading, and physical exam.

2. While in the ER

   Generally, all ERs do a fine job. The problem lies not in what they do but in not making well-organized decisions to admit, observe longer, or discharge. This shortfall stems not from any lack of ability on the part of the ER staff but from a generally poor understanding of opioid addiction and the profound number of variables involved.

3. Now the hard part—deciding when to admit or discharge to home

Every criterion for admission or discharge you will read now is based on published case reports or study. These are not my ideas; I just put them all in one place.

After the patient is given Narcan or flumazenil and the patient is breathing and awake, we continue to evaluate. There are some reasons to admit to the hospital even if the patient is awake and alert. I have selected reasons based on data about which patients eventually wound up in the ICU or needed admission or even died soon. Clearly these patients needed to be admitted. Admit all over-dose patients to the hospital *if* they

- have a seizure any time
- have pink sputum
- have an abnormal CXR
- display a pulse ox of less than 92 percent, while respiratory rate is above twelve
- present a capnography above 50 percent with RR above twelve
- show persistent confusion
- exhibit paranoia
- ever show a GCS below eight, even if only in the field and checked by paramedics
- showed a GCS of less than fifteen at a time of decision-making
- vomit in the field or ER
- do not have a witnessed time of overdose
- could have ingested tricyclic meds
- are older than thirty
- exhibit a Brugada EKG or any abnormal EKG
- are suffering from hypo or hyperthermia

- had to be sedated in the field, for agitation
- overdose with *any* oral agent
- show any sign of fentanyl or methadone use, even if it's just sedation with a negative tox screen
- show abnormal troponin, total creatinine kinase or new renal impairment or abnormal CBC not explained otherwise
- have a respiratory rate greater than twenty or less than ten
- have a heart rate less than fifty or greater than one hundred
- responded to Narcan, but their tox screens were negative for narcotics; it's a sign that a synthetic narcotic is onboard
- required more than nine-tenths of a milligram of Narcan in the ER

Note: It is very easy to overlook some of these things.

If all these criteria are not met and admission is not required, we decide on discharge. But we need another set of criteria to be met before we can actually let our patients go home:

Consider discharge from the ER if

- none of the above criteria is met
- at least nine hours have passed since the last Narcan dose was given or drip was shut off
- patients are awake and alert *without* tactile or verbal stimuli
- patients are able to get up and walk without assistance
- GCS measurement is fifteen
- room air O_2 sat is above 92 percent
- respiratory rates are between eleven and nineteen breaths per minute
- heart rates are between fifty-one and ninety-nine beats per minute

- chest x-rays, repeated eight hours after the last Narcan doses are given, are normal, or document of repeated lung exams are normal
- all logistics and a social-support network are established as in the following section

4. When the overdose patient meets discharge criteria, a social-support network is needed to improve discharge outcome. An ER cannot be expected to produce a social-support team for a drug user. However, with little effort, a great improvement in short-term outcome can be made with the following simple steps, which a person at the ER can be placed in charge of:

- Establish a responsible party and an alternative, two people. These persons can be friends or family. They are responsible for the patient for the next twenty-four hours, and they sign an agreement for this. On a weekend, the responsible parties must sign to be responsible until Monday morning.
- Train them to take pulse rate and respiratory rate and how to use a Narcan kit.
- Provide a Narcan kit either directly or via EScribe, if it is covered by insurance. The responsible party must have the kit in hand at the time of discharge.
- Establish that they have a working cell phone.
- Establish that they have a safe place to take the patient for twenty-four hours.
- Provide a list with contact info for area recovery centers.
- Contact three area recovery centers, and provide that cell number and patient contact info.
- If the patient wishes to enter an in-patient recovery program at this time, keep the patient in the hospital until he or she is contacted by one of the centers.

The ER discharge process and policies will need further improvements that are not yet available. To bring this about, we will need continued research and development.

Near-Future Research and Development

- Insurance payers need to be responsible for paying for full admissions if requested by ER doctors. There must be no denials.
- NIDA must be tasked with timely development of bedside blood tests for every drug of abuse, particularly the fentanyl analogs, W-15, and K2 at first, and then other substances as they become known.
- Data on outcomes from this protocol must be kept for feedback and changes to the protocol.
- Direct admit from ER to rehab protocol and policy need development, especially for patients with no family support.
- National development of this protocol and data from it needs to be freely available online to all hospitals and personnel.

A-39
Discussion of stopping off-label use of narcotics

I want to start this section by explaining what "off-label" use of a medicine is. The best way to do this is to explain what "on-label" use is first. If you're a doctor, you will not need to read this whole section.

When a new medicine is invented, the manufacturer will study its effect on a given illness. For example, if we developed a new blood-pressure medicine, we would give the medicine to patients with high blood pressure and then check to see if the pressure goes down. If the pressure goes down, that's good. We would also look for bad side effects.

Let's look at some common blood-pressure medicine, a calcium-channel blocker. One calcium-channel blocker is called amlodipine, and another is verapamil. Another type of blood-pressure medicine is lisinopril. Lisinopril is an angiotensin converting enzyme (ACE) inhibitor-type medicine. When we study these three medicines, we give them to many different types of patients. When we give these medicines to patients with weak hearts, we find varying results. Amlodipine seems to be OK for these heart patients, verapamil makes them sicker, and lisinopril makes them better, actually improving heart function. We also see that patients with kidney failure suffer bad effects on their kidneys from lisinopril but not from amlodipine or verapamil.

The manufacturer will say that verapamil is "not indicated" for heart-failure patients. In the data sheets published for these medicines, a doctor can find warnings and cautions about when not to use them. For verapamil six serious reactions are listed in the data sheet along with six indications. These six indications are illnesses that have been treated and studied carefully and are well known to improve through the use of verapamil. If a doctor prescribes verapamil for an illness that is not listed among the indications, the doctor is using the medicine off label. It doesn't mean he or she is doing something wrong; it does mean that the FDA did not review any study and approve your particular illness for treatment with this medicine. The doctor may have a very good study with great data to show that this medicine is also good for your illness—or the doctor *may not*. I use medicine off label every day, but I first make sure that I have a good study that shows that it is safe and effective and that I have no safer alternative.

Let me give you an example. If you have a bleeding stomach ulcer, your doctor will want you to take a medicine to stop the production of stomach acid, which will allow the stomach to heal its ulcer and stop bleeding. You may be asked to take a double dose of a medicine that will greatly lower your stomach acid. When the doctor finds that the ulcer is healed, you may be told to go back to only one pill a day.

We have many good studies showing that this double dose is good and safe. But the FDA did not study this, so it is still called an off-label use of the medicine. And, it is important to note, your insurance company may refuse to pay for the two pills per day because it does not pay for off-label uses.

Your insurance company will likely pay for high-dose NSAID medicine, which can give you a stomach ulcer; for verapamil, even if you have heart failure; or for lisinopril, even if you have kidney trouble. The insurance company makes decisions based only on FDA approval for this expensive stomach medicine, to save money, even though we have studies that show the double dose will heal an ulcer. But for cheap medicine like lisinopril and verapamil, they don't seem to care about off-label use. Once again, we see an elaborate system that seems to be designed to protect you from a dangerous doctor, but it really is designed to save someone else's money.

Having seen the difference between an indicated use of a medicine approved by the FDA and an off-label use that is well studied and safe but not reviewed by the FDA, let's look at other types of usages. Here is another example: A problem today in hospitals is the development of MRSA pneumonia. This is a lung infection caused by a staph bacterium that cannot be killed by many antibiotics. We have, however, three good antibiotics that kill MRSA; they are vancomycin, daptomycin, and linezolid. Daptomycin is easy and safe to use, so if you get MRSA pneumonia (a lung infection) and your doctor starts you on daptomycin, that sounds fine. But despite this medicine working on bloodstream infection, it is known to be ineffective in lung infections. This is not a case of off-label use but of what I call "known ineffective use." It won't hurt you, but it doesn't help.

What would happen if you gave testosterone to a patient who's had prostate surgery for hypertrophy? It would make the prostate worse. Suppose you gave estrogen to a woman with ER-positive breast cancer or a history of uterine cancer. It would worsen the cancer. This is what we call "contraindicated use" (known to possibly cause harm). Then we could add another level of use of a drug: one that will hurt you because you are known to be allergic to it.

So the spectrum of use is as follows:

A. Indicated
B. Off-label
C. Known to be ineffective
D. Contraindicated
E. Known to have been previously harmful

You could add a level B-2 off-label but only show *some* help/efficacy, which could describe a rare chemotherapy attempted as a last-ditch effort to save a cancer patient.

How does all this new knowledge you have fit into the context of our drug-overdose epidemic? What is going on *now* with regard to studies about narcotics, and FDA approvals versus what doctors actually do with medicines? Can pharmaceutical companies do studies and make it look like given drugs are safe and effective when they are not? Yes, they can. A publication can also contain an article written to make a drug look bad when it is not. No one is perfect. And these studies are hard to do. Many draw the wrong conclusion.

Let me give you an example of how, in my opinion, a company can make a drug look good when it's not. The most common way is through a practice called "data dilution." When we study a drug, we use the drug to fight a given illness and see what the results are. Did it work or not? It sounds simple, but we can make a mess of it, too. Let's consider a new anti-biotic to fight strep-throat infection. We simply give the new medicine to, say, one hundred people with strep throat. We also give an old antibiotic like penicillin to another one hundred people with strep throat, and we compare results. If all one hundred on the new antibiotic get better, but only ninety in the penicillin group get better, then we say the new drug is better than penicillin.

In real life it's not that simple. We must look at adverse reactions, too. If twenty-five people in the new antibiotic group got diarrhea that required hospitalization, then the new drug helped seventy-five and hurt twenty-five while the old drug helped ninety and hurt no one. So the old drug is better. I'm sure you can think of other scenarios that could happen.

What if the new drug did cure all the patients, but one died from some other strange reaction to the drug? Would you say the new drug helped ninety-nine and the old drug helped ninety, so the new drug is better? Of course not. You would want to know why that one person died. You would want another investigation before allowing the new antibiotic to be sold on the market.

Now let's look at a real-life example of how a company in my opinion can use data dilution to make its drug seem safe *and* how doctors can react wrongly to new medical data. A popular new arthritis and joint-pain medicine was introduced. It was found to cause 30 percent fewer stomach ulcers than older medicines. Because doctors knew that the older medicines could cause stomach ulcers, they used it only when absolutely necessary, and when they heard of the new, safer medicine, they used that one much more frequently. But it was only 30 percent safer, so when I worked in a hospital I saw many more stomach ulcers than ever before. If it's 30 percent safer, but you prescribe it 100 percent more, where do you end up? You guessed it: you end up with even more ulcers. (Example math: If one hundred prescriptions of the old medicine cause ten ulcers, then two hundred prescriptions of the new medicine will cause fourteen ulcers.)

Do you see how complex this all is, even with me keeping it in lay terms?

Now let's look at data dilution and, again, how it was used, in my opinion. This same medicine was felt to cause heart attacks, so the manufacturer was told to study the problem. One would expect to see a study comparing the old medicine to the new one in two equal groups of patients and simply counting heart-attack rates to compare the two meds. Instead, the company gave the new medicine to one thousand patients and then also gave the old medicine to another thousand, and they counted the "*combined* endpoints" of heart attack and arrhythmia. That means that if a patient had a heart attack, it was counted as bad, and if another patient had an arrhythmia, that patient was put into the same bad group. Thus, the term "combined end points" of heart attack and arrhythmia. Any time you combine two things, you dilute each of them, don't you? Now look at the math.

We saw numbers about like this. The new med produced one hundred arrhythmias and six heart attacks, totaling 106 endpoints. The old med produced one hundred arrhythmias and three heart attacks, for a total of 103 endpoints. The scores of 106 and 103 are less than 3 percent different, so they are considered "the same." *But* no one ever said the new med caused arrhythmia, so I question why they combined the endpoints like that. If you look only at heart attack, you see a score of six to three, or a 100 percent difference. The new medicine seems to have an effect on heart attacks, in my opinion.

Again, back to our opioid epidemic. Simply stated, older studies on how to use narcotic pain medicine are filled with problems like this to such an extent that they are useless by today's standards. They combined many types of pain into one, whereas we now know that narcotics do not work on all types of pain. In particular, we know that they do not work well at all on neuropathic pain. There have never been any studies done on patients' functionality while on the meds. The patients who got addicted and hurt by the meds were not included properly in the data. We now have many new studies that show what *not* to use the narcotics on. But pharma sales representatives don't show these studies to doctors, nor does the FDA redo its work to properly classify true indications or dosages for opioids.

So the situation now is this: If we look at only FDA-approved indications for narcotics, then most doctors are doing things correctly. *But* if a good doctor who has expertise in pain control and is up-to-date on all the latest studies uses these medicines, he will use lower doses and use narcotics less. Having been in medicine for many years and having seen many changes, this is all very simple to me. As time goes on and a given field of medicine gets more complex, we develop specific training, and a new specialty is developed. The older doctor will remember when there was no such thing as an ICU. Now we have special ICU doctors. The same is true for every specialty.

The time has come regarding pain medicine to reopen all files for reevaluation of all the proper indications for the use of narcotics and not allow just any doctor to use these medicines for any type of pain in any doses that he or she want to. Let's look at all the latest studies that show that narcotics—that is, opioids—don't work on all types of pain nor at any dose you want. The time is here to *relabel* these medicines and to stop allowing off-label use. It will prevent a great deal of overprescribing.

To recap: Collect and become familiar with all the new studies. Relabel for proper indications and dosages. And no longer allow off-label use of these medicines.

Remember, if the medicine works and solves your pain, then you don't get addicted to it. You simply use it, and it works as intended. But if an opioid is used for a type of pain that will only be partly relieved, then the patient will try more and more medicine with no better results, and addiction will result.

Again, a national computer system would track and control this. By entering diagnoses into the computer, a doctor will invoke the proper dosages and controls on narcotic prescriptions. And the computer can educate both doctor and patient about safer alternatives. This is *exactly* what your insurance company does now, when a doctor writes a prescription for an expensive medicine. The company computer will reject it and will send a letter or fax to the doctor asking that a cheaper alternative medicine be used. Here again are engineering roadblocks for the sake of a company's money but none on patient safety.

FUNDING SOURCES FOR THE DRUG-ABUSE DEATH-REDUCTION PLAN DATABASE

The fundamental principle behind funding the program without taxes involves reorganizing NIDA's budget (NIDA's current budget is more than $1 billion a year and does not produce ideal results) or using the fee system much the same as any other professional licensure system. Some suggestions are detailed below.

- A 1 percent surcharge on $9 billion in narcotics sales in the United States would generate $90 million.
- Nine hundred thousand doctors in the United States paying only $100 per year would generate $90 million.
- Fifty-six thousand pharmacies in the United States paying a $500 fee would generate $28 million.
- Four thousand pharmaceutical companies in the United States paying $10,000 each would generate $40 million.
- The 2,909,357 nurses in the United States paying just $25 each would generate $72,733,925.
- Hospitals could be charged fees by their numbers of beds, in the interest of fair treatment to smaller hospitals. But charging 924,333 hospital beds just a base price of $100 each would generate $92,433,300.
- The eighty-six thousand physician assistants and nurse practitioners in the United States paying $50 each would generate $4.3 million.

This plan contains a prescription-monitoring website that doctors are required to use. Advertising could be sold on it at a premium, because every doctor in the United States would be using this site. Just one dollar a minute for each state (50 × 60 × 24 × 365) would generate $26,280,000 annually.

A grand total of more than $443,680,000 would be generated, which is more than enough to run the program with no new taxes. And after start-up, the advertising charges alone may sustain it.

SOME CLOSING REMARKS

Now that you have read my plan, you can decide to support or reject it. If you reject the plan, it means you support not initiating the recommended controls—which means you share at least some of the following thoughts. I will apologize in advance for insulting anyone with these remarks, but this is my last chance to drive these points home. I feel strongly about saving lives and that no one should die this way.

- You want doctors to write narcotics prescriptions to patients even if the patients already have prescriptions from other doctors.
- You don't care if doctors give patients overdoses of narcotics and completely disregard known ceiling-effect-safe doses.
- You think it's OK for hospitals to give patients narcotics prescriptions even if the patients already have them at home.
- You don't want to penalize a hospital or doctor for overdosing patients.
- You think a drug misuser should have power over a hospital and bring fines on the hospital if the hospital doesn't give the misuser whatever he or she wants.
- You think that a person who has leftover narcotics should give them to a friend.
- You don't want to know which drugs are killing people.
- You want anyone who wants to, to print prescription blanks on any kind of paper desired, so drug dealers can copy them on Photoshop.
- You think it's OK for someone to get a narcotic prescription that is not needed and then sell the pills in schools to children.
- You think it's OK for persons to buy prescriptions from their friends.
- You think that if a doctor is caught selling prescriptions, he or she won't do it again.
- You want NIDA to spend $1.3 billion of your tax money every year with no reduction in overdoses to show for it.

- You think that cocaine is fascinating.
- You want children to graduate from high school knowing nothing about dangerous drugs.
- You don't care that 150 people died today from drug abuse; you just want the weather on the news.
- You want to spend more tax money on drugs.
- You don't care whether we monitor the effects of a new program to see if it works or not.
- You think it's OK that the child sitting next to yours in school has little control on the drugs in his or her pocket.
- You don't care if children are exposed to ads for harmful substances at the school-bus stop.
- You think it's OK to crush and snort oxycodone pills.
- You think it's OK that a child can learn how to snort narcotics by watching a video about it on YouTube.
- You think it's OK for social media to show all of America how to do drugs.
- You think it's OK for a doctor to take cash from a patient for narcotics prescriptions and then bill Medicare for lab tests and x-rays for the same patient.
- If in your neighborhood, a person killed multiple people by selling them drugs, you don't want to know.
- You want the patent office to be funded by your tax dollars to publish how to make drugs on line.
- You want the NIDA to use your tax money to invent drugs like K2 that will kill kids.
- You want to sell designer drugs at local stores and smoke shops.
- You think it's cool if kids go into neighborhood trash to get used fentanyl patches and eat them.
- You want doctors to mail narcotics scripts to patients who can't get to the office.
- You want hospitals to always treat your pain, even if it kills you.

- Even though a board-certified pain-control doctor may not be able to control a patient's pain after years of trying, you want to punish an ER doctor who finds that he or she cannot do so within one visit in the ER.
- You think it's OK if a doctor issues 423 narcotics prescriptions every day.
- You don't want safe pain medicine.
- You want your insurance carrier and hospital to offer you the cheapest possible drugs, not necessarily the safest ones.
- You want a hospital CEO to determine what your doctor is allowed to give you, in order to save the CEO money.
- If a person has trouble stopping a narcotic, you don't care; let him or her go through withdrawal or just switch to heroin.

ATTITUDE IS EVERYTHING

Who first said this? Google it, and you will find many answers. I would like to say that too much attitude can be a big problem. Consider the high-ranking government spokesperson who opined that drug addicts need more willpower, not more help. This is an overwhelming statement that seems to me to show that this person places 100 percent of the blame for the opioid epidemic on addicts themselves. This is horrifying to me. The person showed a lack of experience, knowledge, and compassion; displayed arrogance toward those who have lost loved ones to the opioid epidemic; and should not be in a position of authority. This person has an attitude problem.

The concept of the attitude problem lies at the heart of efforts to stop the epidemic. Understanding this will help you make good choices, which will lead to the saving of lives.

I do not refer to addiction as a disease. Arguing over a name will not save lives. But it is a societal problem. Let me show you a parallel society, its problem, and the similarities between the two societies. And let us look for solutions to our problems.

Consider the Native American tribe known as the Tohono O'odham. Until 1960 no members of the tribe had diabetes. After 1960 the population started eating a new diet that included rich foods high in sugar and fat instead of their traditional diet of seeds, grains, and some meat. This modern-world diet gave them diabetes. Or did it? What do you think? If the diet did this, then is diabetes a disease in the eyes of the tribe? Those who still eat their traditional diet don't have diabetes. The new diet was brought to them from another place. They didn't crave it when they didn't know about it. If they now allow their children to grow up eating candy, cake, refined sugar, fatty food, and ice cream, they will have a diabetes epidemic. In summary, we are looking at a nation of people who never had what we refer to as a disease until new substances were introduced to them. Or consider that this new substance is capable of overwhelming their willpower, like giving them a disease. Our own president (Obama) said, "I can't stop smoking." Isn't that addiction?

Opioid drugs are the mind's candy. Remember that even NIDA indicates that they "enhance pleasure" and "have a fascinating effect on the brain."

Why would a senior White House official, a person who regularly confers with the president, say that drug addicts just need more willpower? (Try to take rich, sugary foods out of the White House; just try it.) The remark completely ignored the fact that we have a company in America manufacturing 163 metric tons yearly of the most addictive drug ever made. Has anyone at the president's conference table ever seen a person high on drugs? The president and his most trusted staff members were well into adulthood when oxycontin became a common substance of abuse. Studies have shown the initial age of onset of substance abuse is eleven for alcohol, twelve for hallucinogens, fourteen for marijuana, sixteen for cocaine; and a large increase in ER visits due to narcotics abuse starts at age eighteen. But opioids were not around when the president and many of his staff members were kids. Neither were cell phones. If you're seventy years old, you likely can't understand why your grandkids won't put their cell phones down. The random nature of information obtainable online and the ease of obtaining it are addicting. It's a new phenomenon, so if you didn't grow up with it, you may not understand it. At one time, we all would ask, "Why would you want to take narcotics? Don't they just put you to sleep?" No, they don't. Even the government agency people whom you paid to study drugs will tell you that narcotics enhance pleasure. Anyone who says that drug use is a function of willpower needs a dictionary to look up "addictive."

Let us recall President Trump's aforementioned meeting with the two young people who were drug addicts; they both told him they started with oxycodone. When asked what it felt like when they took the drug for the first time, one said, "I knew I always wanted to feel like that all the time."

Trump responded, "I had no idea." He said it himself. On national TV in front of senior White House staff, who included the attorney general, the person who made the comment about willpower, and the secretary of the Department of Health and Human Services, when a US president was told that young people were starting with oxycodone and then moving on to heroin, he admitted that he "had no idea" how addictive the drug was. Yet none of these same people has answered my letters detailing my plan. They are not listening.

Narcotics have been known to be addictive for fifteen hundred years. And the United States makes 359,414 pounds of it yearly without a single engineering control on its distribution or sale.

ACKNOWLEDGMENTS

I wish to express my sincere gratitude to the many people, ranging from doctors, nurses, police officers, DEA agents, family, and friends, who have freely provided their thoughts and ideas to contribute to this plan and to the families of those whose loss of life has inspired me to continue this work rather than relax on my days off. Special thanks to Senator Tim Kaine for his interest in saving lives.

I cannot begin to express my deep regret about the countless government officials who haven't even replied to my letters.

Terence Schiller, MD: FightDrugsNow@gmail.com

Made in the USA
Columbia, SC
31 May 2019